WORKING WITH CHILDREN
DEVELOPING A CURRICULUM
FOR THE EARLY YEARS

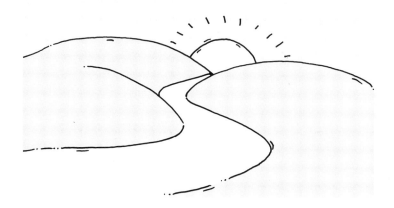

A learning pack for people who work with young children

MARY JANE DRUMMOND, MARGARET LALLY AND GILLIAN PUGH
(editors)
on behalf of a group including
Peter Heaslip, Jennie Lindon, Jane Petzing and Susan Williams

UNDER FIVES UNIT
NATIONAL CHILDREN'S BUREAU

© 1989

NOTE ON THE EDITORS

Mary Jane Drummond, Tutor in Primary Education, Cambridge Institute of Education

Margaret Lally, Development Officer, Under Fives Unit, National Children's Bureau

Gillian Pugh, Head, Under Fives Unit, National Children's Bureau

Other publications from the National Children's Bureau:

Working Towards Partnership in the Early Years   Gillian Pugh and Erica De'Ath   1989

Services for Under Fives: developing a co-ordinated approach   Gillian Pugh   1988

Working with Parents: a training resource pack   Erica De'Ath and Gillian Pugh (editors)   1986

Please contact:-
National Children's Bureau,
8 Wakley Street,
London EC1V 7QE
Telephone 01 278 9441

CONTENTS

IMPORTANT

This symbol appears on those pages which may be reproduced, photocopied, etc.

All other pages are covered by copyright and may not be reproduced without permission from the publisher

ACKNOWLEDGEMENTS

This pack of training materials has been edited by Mary Jane Drummond (Cambridge Institute of Education) and Gillian Pugh and Margaret Lally (Under Fives Unit at the National Children's Bureau), on behalf of a group that met at the National Children's Bureau over an 18 month period during 1987 - 1988. Members of the group have included Peter Heaslip (Bristol Polytechnic), Jennie Lindon (research psychologist and NNEB), Jane Petzing (Norfolk LEA), and Susan Williams (Preschool Playgroups Association).

Others who have contributed to the pack are Phillip Gammage (Nottingham University), Helen Green (NSPCC family centre, London), Neil Kitson (Northamptonshire LEA), Katey Mairs (Pen Green Centre, Corby), Carol Tomlinson (High/Scope Development Officer) Judith Woodhead (teacher and parent), and Jethyn Hall (Montessori Society).

This final version of the pack is the result of developmental testing of about 150 draft copies in schools and classes, playgroups, family centres and day nurseries, and training courses all over the country. We are indebted to all those who have fed back their comments to us as we have been revising the pack for publication.

We would particularly like to thank:

Win Amatiello, Ann Buffham, Faith Davey, Christine Menzies and Sally Whittingham, Bristol;

Jane Bond, Wincobank Nursery;

Helen Brown, Lancashire LEA;

Marilyn Richardson, St Bernadettes RC Primary School, Blackpool;

Sheila Johnson, Clough Fold County Primary School, Skelmersdale; and staff in Lancashire schools;

Chatteris Early Years Group, Cambridgeshire;

Shirley Cleave, Sandra Brown and Caroline Sharp, National Foundation for Educational Research;

J Dowden and staff and volunteers at RAF Marham Nursery School, Norfolk;

Marion Dowling and Dawn Bishop, Dorset LEA and staff at Hamworthy First School, Poole;

Malmesbury Park First School, Kingsleigh First School, Elmrise First School and Summerbee First School, Bournemouth;

Heathlands First School, Venwood CE First School, Somerford Infants School and Christ the King School, Dorset;

Naomi Eisenstadt and Nicky Road, Save the Children Fund ;

M Grant, Park Lane County Primary School, Peterborough;

Helen Green and colleagues at Oxford Gardens NSPCC Family Centre, London;

Julia Gilkes, Canterbury Children's Centre, Bradford;

Elizabeth Gregson, Seven Sisters Infant School, Tottenham;

Pat Heaslip and staff at Bluebell Valley Nursery, Bristol;

Margaret Heritage, Warwickshire LEA;

Sue Hill, Jubilee Family centre, Leicester;

Annette Holman, Strathclyde Pre-Fives Unit;

Shirley Humpleby, Dewsbury College;

Patricia Kent and staff at Truro Nursery School, Cornwall;

Peggy McConchie and C Tucker and CPQS students at Hounslow Borough College;

Kate Morris, Middlesborough General Hospital;

Hilary Pursehouse and staff at Columbia Market Nursery School, Tower Hamlets;

Ann Sharp, Glenys Swift, Kath Hirst, Ann Hedley, Lynda Hill, Cathy Nutbrown, Sheffield LEA;

Iram Siraj-Blatchford, Essex Institute of Higher Education;

Gordon Turner and colleagues, Schools Curriculum Development Council;

Wendy Suschitzky and colleagues, Shree Ram Krishna Centre, Loughborough;

Marilyn Wilson, Sharrow Junior School;

June Wood and staff at Madeley Nursery School, Shropshire,

and all the many teachers, nursery nurses, playgroup leaders, parents and students who were involved in meetings to work on and discuss parts of the pack.

Acknowledgement to Croom Helm for permission to reprint the extract from *Education Under Six* by Denison Deasey and to Methuen Educational for permission to reprint the extract from *Susan Isaacs:The first biography* by D.E.M. Gardner.

A warm thank you to Patsy Archibald and Dido Whitehead who have patiently typed up several versions of the pack.

Finally our thanks to the Department of Health and the Department of Education and Science for funding the work of the Under Fives Unit; and to the National Children's Play and Recreation Unit for a generous grant which helped towards the production of this pack.

Section 1
INTRODUCTION

INTRODUCTION

WHY HAS THIS PACK BEEN DEVELOPED?

Early childhood is not just a period when children are prepared and trained for adult life: it is a time of development and growth that is important in its own right. All children have the right to spend their early years in an environment that will foster all aspects of their development. Those who work with young children in group settings outside the home have taken on the responsibility of providing such an environment: it is a challenging and demanding undertaking.

This pack has been developed to support early years workers in nurseries, schools, playgroups, day nurseries and family centres, who want to work together to examine their present practice, their ideals, their aspirations and their projects for the future.

IT AIMS TO HELP WORKERS

- be clearer about what they are trying to achieve in their work with young children

- develop their skills of observing children

- explore the complex process of young children's learning

- look critically at their own role in supporting children's learning

- look at the values that underpin their work

The pack is not a ready-made curriculum handbook, nor an early years version of the National Curriculum. It is made up of activities that will help early years workers understand more about the curriculum that they now provide,and that will support them as they try to develop more effective practice.

The values and attitudes that we bring to our workplaces have a powerful impact on the children in our charge. Throughout the pack reference is made to issues of racism and sexism, and to the fact that we live in a multi-cultural society. All workers with young children, including those working in predominantly or all white areas, have a responsibility to identify and examine racist and sexist attitudes and practices.

This is a challenging time for early years workers, and it is important that they are given time and opportunities to think about, discuss and plan the work that they do. This pack has been produced to support that thinking.

USING THE PACK

USERS' COMMENTS

We learned to work together - share ideas - develop trust - grow in confidence - learn about other people's workplaces.

We learned that *how* you work with people - enabling them to participate - is as important as the content of what you are discussing.

We allowed discussion to develop to meet the needs of individuals.

Doing a course using the pack really gave us time to think.

Mixed groups - of workers from different backgrounds - were particularly good.

It made me look in depth at my daily work.

It helped to stress the need to examine and question assumptions.

I learned that motivation is increased by group members setting their own goals.

I learned that there is no correct way of organising the curriculum - each school/playgroup/nursery/worker has to find their own answer.

It worked well because it drew on people's own personal experience.

2

WHO WILL USE THE PACK?

The pack has been designed as a set of resources for you to select from. Each section has clearly defined purposes and each activity has been devised to give you and your colleagues certain experiences. But please do not feel that you have to start at activity 3A and work through every activity to the end of section 10! It is worth reading through the whole pack before the course or your training day, but how you plan your work and which activities you select will depend on you - on the needs of your particular group and the time you have available.

THE PACK CAN BE USED

by groups of staff working in similar settings, for example playgroup leaders in one district, or teachers and nursery nurses in a local education authority

by groups of staff working in one locality but in different settings, for example family centre workers, teachers, nursery nurses and playgroup leaders in one town

by a staff team in one nursery or group or centre, for example all the staff in an infant school or day nursery or children's centre

by a committee and staff in a playgroup or parent and toddler group

by members of a local under fives liaison group

by college tutors running post-experience and in-service training courses

by teachers of older children, in a primary or special school

by parents and workers from a nursery or family centre

YOU COULD USE THIS PACK

on a term's course of say ten two-hour evening sessions

on short informal courses of five or six meetings

as support material for regular staff meetings

as a unit of 120 hours on a CPQS course

on a one day multi-disciplinary course for local early years workers

on a school's training day or 'Baker day'

The activities in the pack have been designed primarily for use in small groups of up to 12 people. If you have a much larger group (for example for a day conference) you will need to break down into smaller groups to work on your selected activities.

The role of the group leader is crucial to how the pack is used. Several of the activities require skilled intervention on the part of the group leader, and these have additional notes in the pack. There are also some notes specifically for group leaders in Section 2. Many groups work well when the leadership is shared by two colleagues. This is often both helpful to the group and supportive to the group leaders.

Remember - the whole purpose of the pack is to encourage participants to examine their values and attitudes and their work with children. There are no right answers! The group leader's role is not to 'instruct' but to enable the group to participate, to think, to draw on their own experience, to reflect and to learn. The activities have been designed to help this happen.

WHAT'S IN THE PACK?

PLEASE NOTE that in the summary of the pack contents that follows, the timing for each activity is only approximate, and is given simply to help you plan your course.

SECTION 2: NOTES TO GROUP LEADERS
looks at the value of group work, the role of the group leader and at how to organise and manage sessions.

SECTION 3: WHAT IS LEARNING?
looks at how we learn as adults and at how children learn.

3A   *Learning lessons* - how we learn as adults and the implications of this for our workplace
30 - 45 minutes

3B   *Looking for evidence* - first steps in observing children's learning
60 minutes

3C   *Observing learning* - making observations in the workplace
45 minutes

3D   *Blockbuster* - the adult's role in listening to children and supporting their learning
60 minutes + 45 minutes

3E   *Six into one won't go* - what is learning, and how can principles be translated into practice in the workplace?
30 minutes + 45 minutes

SECTION 4: WHAT DO WE MEAN BY CURRICULUM?
looks at the experiences and activities that make up the curriculum and at the 'hidden curriculum'.

4A   *What is a curriculum made of?* - how much of what happens in your workplace is part of the curriculum?
45 minutes

4B   *That's lovely Raymond* - how we praise or criticise children is one aspect of the 'hidden curriculum'
45 minutes + 30 - 45 minutes

4C   *What does our curriculum look like?* - a review of what you do in your own workplace
45 - 60 minutes

SECTION 5: WHY DO WE DO WHAT WE DO?
examines the experiences in our lives that affect what we bring to the workplace.

5A   *What do we feel is important for learners?* - looking at the skills and experiences we actually provide for a particular child, asking why we feel that they are appropriate
30-40 minutes

5B   *What did we learn in childhood?* - how have the key experiences of our childhood influenced our work with children?
30-40 minutes

5C   *I'll never forget old so and so* - which individuals in our past lives have particularly influenced our thinking?
45 minutes

5D   *Principal principles?* - assessing the importance in our work of the ideas, values and principles of some of the pioneers of early childhood education
90 minutes

5E   *Other people's classrooms and workplaces* - using examples from Susan Issacs and Maria Montessori, this activity looks at how our basic principles affect our work
75 minutes

5F   *Flexibility and change* - how can we be flexible and responsive to changes in society? 60 minutes

SECTION 6: WHAT DO WE BELIEVE IN?

looks at how our personal values affect our work with children, and at how young children acquire values.

6A	*My mother said, I never should ...* - our own early learning	20 minutes
6B	*Rules and regulations* - a look at same implicit values	45 minutes
6C	*Images of childhood* - looking at how society values children	30 - 45 minutes
6D	*Finding out where you stand* - beginning to make values explicit	30 - 45 minutes
6E	*How have I changed?* - how do values change and develop?	45 - 60 minutes
6F	*Professional or personal?* - looking at values in action	45 - 60 minutes
6G	*What is good practice?* - exploring further into underlying values in our practice	90 minutes
6H	*Making difficult decisions* - working with people with different values	30 minutes per case study
6I	*Values in conflict* - how we handle difference and disagreement	45 minutes

SECTION 7: APPROACHES TO THE CURRICULUM

examined in the light of how we plan our own work.

7A	*A child's eye view* - observing a child in detail	45 - 60 minutes
7B	*What's relevant to me?* - a critical look at five different approaches to the curriculum (High/Scope, Rudolf Steiner, Montessori, structured pre-planned lessons, and Portage)	As long as you like
7C	*Curriculum tombola* - using the curriculum framework offered in *Curriculum Matters 2* to examine the curriculum in our own workplaces	30 minutes at any session
7D	*Examining local guidelines* - a look at guidelines produced by local authorities	30 - 60 minutes

5

SECTION 8: OBSERVING CURRENT PRACTICE
focusses on why and how we observe individual children and how we might use these observations.

8A *Preparing to observe* - what is observation, and how can we do it on a more regular basis?
30 minutes

8B *Finding questions of your own* - what do we want to observe, and what questions should we be asking?
30 - 45 minutes

8C *Why? What? How? Who?* - a more detailed look at planning observations
45 - 60 minutes

8D *Curriculum in Action* - six fundamental questions as a framework for observation and evaluation
6 - 10 hours

8E *After questions, what next....?* planning ahead
20 minutes or the rest of your life!

SECTION 9: MOVING FROM AIMS TO PRACTICE
looks at where we want to go in our work with children, at our aims and goals, and at how we move forward and monitor progress.

9A *Design a Poster* - summing up in 15 words the aims of your nursery or centre or group
20 - 30 minutes

9B *Defining goals* - what will our aims look like in practice?
Several sessions of 45 minutes

9C *Reviewing resources and roles* - achieving our goals will depend on what resources we have available and who is going to do what
30 - 40 minutes per goal

9D *Monitoring progress* - looking at how we can ensure we are making progress in achieving our goals
Several sessions of 30 - 40 minutes

SECTION 10: LOOKING BACK AND LOOKING AHEAD
is a review section which gives the opportunity to reflect on the experiences of using the pack.

10A *Reviewing your work with the pack*
30 - 45 minutes

10B *What next?* - what will your next steps be?
30 minutes - or as long as you have got

SECTION 11 is a selected Bibliography of useful books and addresses.

FINDING YOUR WAY AROUND

The pack encourages you to explore your present practice critically by considering four fundamental questions:

Where are we now?
Where do we want to go?
How will we get there?
Should we/can we record our curriculum in writing?

Approaches to these questions are developed through sections 3 - 9 of the pack, which has been designed so that you are free to find your own starting points and routes through the activities, depending on the time available to you, and on your particular interests and concerns.

The best place to begin may well be with the first question
Where are we now?

This can be tackled in a variety of ways, depending on what parts of your present practice you feel you would like to examine in more detail.

As you ask yourself 'Where are we now?', other questions will spring to mind: use these further questions to help you decide which sections to work on.

For example:

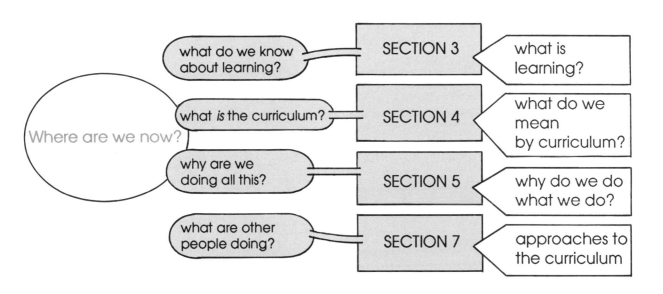

If you have plenty of time, you may want to work through each of these sections in turn. Or, you may decide to select a few activities from each section, starting with section 3 or 4, and moving on to section 5 or 7. Or you may prefer a more meandering route through these sections. There is no need to feel that you must complete any one section before starting on another: there are many possibilities, and you are free to change direction at any time.

Neither of these possibilities should be seen as a route you are *obliged* to follow. You will quickly discover which sections of the pack are the most rewarding and stimulating for you.

Two possible pathways:

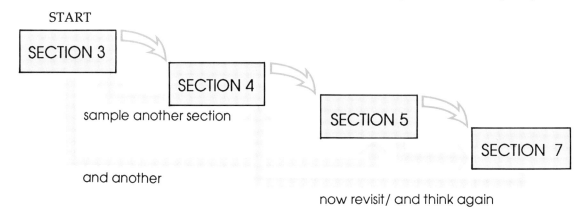

Later in your work with the pack, as further questions arise in your discussions, you may want to revisit some or all of these sections.

After some work on the first question, you may want to move on to the second basic question Where do we want to go?

This question can be approached through working through some of the activities in sections 5 and 7. Again, use your own interests, concerns and priorities to help you plan your work.

For example:

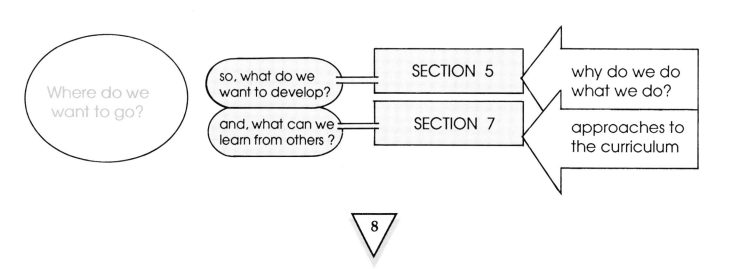

8

Rather than completing one section before moving on to the next,
you may choose to move fairly freely between the two sections.

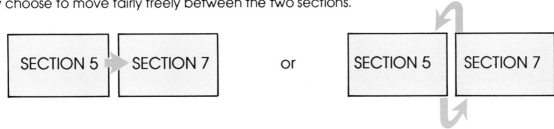

The third question How will we get there? follows on from thinking about 'Where do we want to go'.
This question is approached in sections 8 and 9, which are designed to follow on from one another.

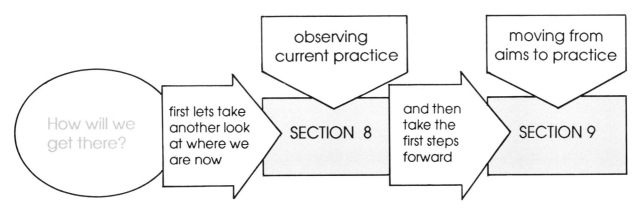

The fourth and final question Should we record our
curriculum in writing? is approached in section 9.

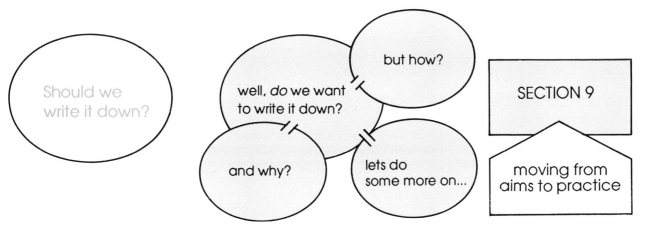

At this point, you may decide you need to return to earlier sections:
arriving at section 9 doesn't necessarily mean that you have
completed all the work you can usefully do.

Section 6: What do we believe in?
This section has rather a different function from the other sections.
In this section you are invited to examine some of the fundamental
values and beliefs that underlie your present practice, your aspirations for the future, and your chosen ways of moving forward. Work
on this section will probably best be undertaken throughout your
work on the pack.

Whenever you catch yourselves asking one of those searching
('What's the meaning of life?') questions about your deeply held
convictions, or when you feel that your discussion could profitably
go a little deeper below the surface, you might consider using one
or more of the activities in section 6.

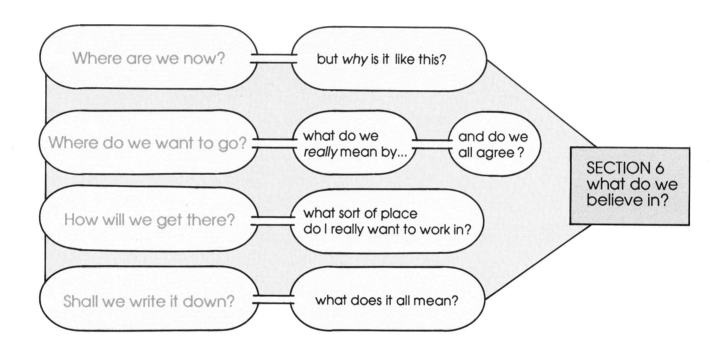

The workshop leader's notes for section 6 will explain that some of
the activities in it may be seen as challenging, even threatening,
by some group members. It may be wise to start work on section 6
only when the group has established an easy-going effective
working relationship: it certainly wouldn't be the best place to start
with a group of people who are new to each other, or who have
had little experience of working together.

Section 10 is a concluding section
Wherever you have got to just before you decide to stop, it will be
worthwhile to look at section 10 Looking back: looking
ahead. This section is important for review, for evaluation, and for
planning what you intend to do next. Perhaps you will decide to
go back to the beginning and start all over again!

A CURRICULUM FOR YOUNG CHILDREN

The word curriculum appears on the cover and title page of this pack, and is also the explicit focus of section 4 What do we mean by curriculum? Since the word is often used to refer to a structured school based programme, many early years workers may consider that the term does not apply to them at all. And now that the National Curriculum has arrived in schools for children aged five and over, the concept may seem even more remote to many workers. But in this pack, the word is used in a rather different way, to refer to the whole range of experiences offered to young children in group settings outside the home. Used in this sense, the curriculum of young children includes

all the opportunities for learning and development that are made available to children

the activities, attitudes and behaviour that are planned, encouraged, tolerated, ignored or forbidden

the way the room is organised and the routines followed by children and adults

the part adults take in organising, directing, influencing and joining in what the children do

the extent to which parents are involved in each of the above

Those working with young children in schools, especially those in reception classes for 4 and 5 year olds in primary schools, may find this description of curriculum a useful one when they join their colleagues in planning to meet, and then implementing, the requirements of the National Curriculum.

Section 2
NOTES FOR GROUP LEADERS

NOTES FOR GROUP LEADERS

1. The value of group work

There are many advantages of working in groups, the greatest of which is the opportunity it provides for *learning from and building on our own experiences.*

The group may act

> *to support active learning* by providing opportunities to learn from each other through tackling problems and tasks cooperatively

> *to reveal hidden strengths* and potential in individuals, where helping and leadership come from members of the group

> *to provide a sounding board* where other people are on hand to listen to our ideas and offer a range of responses and give opinions

> *to give emotional support,* by helping people to value their own ideas and experiences and alleviate feelings of isolation

> *to recognise that most people have worries* or anxieties and feelings of inadequacy and to share ways of overcoming or coping with them

> *to promote participation,* with openness and sharing in the group acting as a model for working more closely with colleagues at work and with parents

However, working in groups can be difficult and there are a number of areas to be careful about and pitfalls to avoid

> *careful planning* is needed to ensure the group tackles the work effectively. Having co-leaders can provide support and help

> *people's expectations and perceptions* of groups are often very different. It is important to clarify the aims of the group at the beginning to diminish anger or disappointment. A short work shop series may not be able to meet all expectations, but a longer series of events could be planned later by the group

> *people's confidence and ability to participate* in groups varies. Some people speak a great deal and others are often silent. All need to be respected

> *some groups can become destructive,* with a highly critical and judgemental atmosphere. It helps to keep the focus on the materials and encourage constructive criticism and positive comments

> *an agreement on confidentiality* should be established within the group before asking for personal sharing amongst members

> *splitting people into pairs and smaller groups* makes it easier for some to participate in the discussion. Clear instructions on what should be reported back to the large group are important, so that key points of discussion are not lost, while individual confidences are respected

2. The role of the group leader

The group leader's task is to enable group members to think and learn, rather then to impart information or to instruct.

This will mean

planning the course as a whole as well as each individual session

relating each session, and the material presented for discussion, *to the experience and the needs* of group members

reviewing and evaluating each session before planning the next

facilitating learning, through listening, encouraging, probing, and consolidating progress

building on the expertise and experience that members bring to the group

challenging group members to look critically at what they do with young children

using questions to help group members to reflect on their assumptions and expectations

clarifying issues in the group and *drawing together* the points made in discussion

Co-leadership

Some people find running groups easier if they work as a pair as co-leaders. It can be very helpful to have someone else to plan sessions with and to review what is happening. Two leaders also offer the opportunity for group members to relate to two different personalities and leadership styles.

Co-leadership is an excellent way of training new group leaders - an apprenticeship model, for someone who has participated in groups and understands the mechanics but needs some support and experience in group leadership.

If co-leadership is chosen, be sure that both people are clear about who is doing what: leading group exercises and activities, chairing open discussion groups or plenary sessions, taking notes. All these tasks can be successfully shared provided that the delegation of responsibilities is made explicit for both people concerned.

3.   Organising sessions

Before the group meetings start

Who is coming? Who will invite or inform them? What is the best size for this group?

What will the overall format of events or activities be? How many, how often and how long will the group meetings be? How much will it cost?

Where will the group meet?

When will it meet - dates and times?

How will the time be organised? Do these events have to fit into a previously structured programme/a staff meeting/a lunch hour?

Who will be involved in making all these decisions and how will the information be made available to others?

The size of the group will be determined by a number of different factors, not least the size of the room(s) available. The materials in this pack have been designed primarily for use in pairs and small groups of up to 12 people who may form part of a much larger group.

It is difficult to have large group discussions with more than 20 people. If you are planning a one day seminar of 60 - 70 people, several experienced leaders will be necessary to allow you to break into smaller work groups.

On arrival

Who will be responsible for:

> welcoming group members
> refreshments
> setting up the furniture/equipment
> starting off the group meeting

Starting off

Even when members of a group already know each other it is important to start the first meeting in a way that is active, welcoming, inclusive of all and demonstrates the participatory and sharing nature of the group.
One way is to ask each group member to talk to his or her neighbour for 4 - 5 minutes and then to introduce each other to the group.
If there is to be a series of meetings the first one should be primarily given over to clarifying the purpose and aims of the group, negotiating an agreed programme , establishing ground rules and identifying what individual members have to offer the group.

The main activities

In planning which activities to include it is important not only to have a clear focus for the session, but also to be prepared to respond to the contributions made by members of the group. Their experience and concerns may mean you have to work more slowly - or more quickly - or re-plan your next session.

If the session is being planned as part of a longer course, or if the group members come from a variety of workplaces , the group leader should act as a resource and a facilitator, rather than participating in the individual exercises. You will need to observe and listen to group members' response to the activities to enable you to 'tune into' their concerns and to help you to match the content of future sessions to the group's needs. However if you are running a session (or series of sessions) within your own workplace with your colleagues, it is important that you take part in the activities and share your experience with the rest of the group.

Establishing rules

It is important to negotiate with the group and establish some working rules before you start. You may want to consider

Group membership: is it an open group with a fluctuating membership or closed, i.e. a certain group of named people only? Are they committed to attend every meeting?

Emphasising a positive and constructive approach: encourage any critical feedback to include an alternative way of behaving.

Using the group to learn from: while nobody should feel forced to take part in any of the activities, group members should be encouraged to take personal responsibility for their learning and use the group to explore new ways of thinking.

Expectations: how will individual expectations be negotiated if they are inconsistent with the group goals and resources?

Confidentiality: all information shared between individuals within the group should be treated as confidential.

Time-keeping: start on time, end on time and agree the use of time between and within group meetings.

Keeping the group 'on task'

The group leader needs to be able to draw on group members'
experience but also to keep the group focussed on the task. This will
mean amongst other things

> moving the group on to the next part of the task at the appropriate time to ensure that all parts
> of the task are tackled. The group may not need to 'finish' every part.

> helping to keep contributions relevant. This may mean intervention, for example when a group
> member has launched into a lengthy, irrelevant anecdote (e.g. by saying 'I'm sorry to interrupt
> you, but I'm not sure that's exactly what we're looking for at the moment. Time is running by,
> and we need to have completed this by.....so I'm afraid I'll have to stop you').

> recording group members' contributions with notes or on the 'flip chart' or large piece of paper
> provided, so everyone is clear about what they have achieved so far.

> handling problems

One of your most challenging tasks will be to resolve difficulties in the
group that threaten to prevent individuals or the group as a whole
from making progress.

These may include

> conflict between two or more strong points of view
>
> prejudice and rigid points of view expressed by any number of group members
>
> different levels of understanding within the group
>
> anger or distress expressed verbally or non-verbally

It is important to confront these and other blocks to learning but not
in such a way that individuals feel threatened or 'put down'.

Some sections, particularly Section 6, are more likely to cause conflict
than others. You will find that the notes for group leaders will alert
you to some potential problems.

If the group seems to be in difficulties caused by conflict, prejudice,
different levels of understanding or rigid points of view it is important
to encourage the group to clarify their thinking and to challenge
themselves, for example

> by asking other group members what they think about what has just been said (e.g. by saying
> 'thank you for sharing that point of view. What about *other* viewpoints in the group?')

> by asking individuals to expand on and clarify their point of view

> by offering articles, videos or other source material which presents a different view - this is par-
> ticularly useful if several forceful members are supporting a rigid point of view

If the group appear to be angry or distressed during the course or
session it is important to address these feelings and try to find out
what has caused the anger or distress. For example was it something
in the session itself, or was it something to do with work which the
session has brought to the surface?

Group members will need to be given time to express their feelings if
the meetings are to continue positively.

Finishing the sessions and the course

There are two parts to finishing a group or series of meetings:
evaluating what has happened and looking ahead to the future.

Evaluation involves considering

> what has been learnt by individual members of the group?
> has the group achieved its goals?
> how did the activities help achieve those goals?
> what helped, hindered, challenged group members?
> what else could the group have done?
> what was missing?

Looking ahead involves considering

> does the group plan to meet again?
> if so, when, why, how?

It is important to take time at the end of every session to reflect with
the group members on what they have been doing, what they have
learned, and difficulties they have experienced.

After a few sessions, group members will probably be secure enough
to express their feeling about the course. This can be a valuable
source of feedback for individuals, for the group and for the group
leaders.

Section 10 of the pack provides an opportunity to reflect on the
pack as a whole, but some of the activities suggested in this section
could be used at intervals throughout a series of meetings, to review
progress so far and plan ahead.

Section 3
WHAT IS LEARNING?

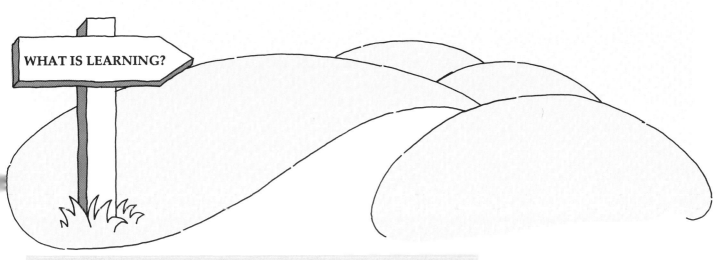

IN WORKING THROUGH THIS SECTION YOU WILL BE ABLE TO

- reflect on your own experiences of learning as an adult

- look at some evidence of young children's learning

- discuss the place that adults play in young children's learning

- work to establish some general principles about learning

- consider how these principles can be translated into practice

USERS' COMMENTS

'This section is a good place to start'

'By looking at our own learning experiences we gained greater understanding of children's problems and difficulties'

LOOKING AT OUR OWN LEARNING

This pack is about adults learning. It has been produced to help us learn about children's learning.

Thinking about ourselves as learners can help in two ways:

we will get better at learning and at supporting the learning of our colleagues

we will understand more about children as learners.

Activity 3A

LEARNING LESSONS   Time 30 - 45 minutes

PREPARATION
Copies of the incomplete sentences below for each group member.

ACTIVITY
1 Spend a few minutes thinking about yourself as an adult learner. For example, how did you learn to use a videorecorder or to drive a car, or to be a parent?

1 Working on your own, complete these sentences
I learn quickly when ....

I learn slowly when ....

I find learning easy when ....

Learning in groups ....

Learning from books ....

I learn well from someone who ....

I enjoy learning when I ....

2 Share your responses with a colleague.   (5 minutes)

What is similar and what is different about your learning patterns?

What do these sentences suggest about your workplace? Is it a good place to learn in? For you and for the children?   (20 minutes)

3 Working in the whole group discuss your conclusions.   (20 minutes)

HOW DO CHILDREN LEARN?

In many ways, very much as we do as adults. The main difference is that because they are younger they have had far fewer experiences. And that means fewer facts on which they can start to build theories about themselves, and the world around them. One way we help children to learn is by providing them with a rich variety of experiences in our workplaces, just as parents do in the home. Another way is to help children, even at a very young age, to think and talk about their experiences. Young children can be helped to think back over what they have just been doing, and to discuss what happened with their friends and with adults. This kind of reflection is an important part of learning.

Activity 3B

LOOKING FOR EVIDENCE

Time 60 minutes

PREPARATION

Group members will need to be asked *in advance* to think back over the last few weeks and select an incident for discussion in the group, as described below.

ACTIVITY

1 Think back over the last few weeks and select a moment when you feel fairly confident that you saw a child in the process of learning something. Bring some piece of concrete evidence of this learning to show your colleagues: it could be anything - a scribble drawing, notes of a conversation with a child, a squashed lunch box.

2 Working in groups of four or five, discuss with your colleagues the reasons for selecting each piece of evidence, and how you came to the conclusion that the children were learning from their experience. Think about the context in which the learning took place - what happened before, during and after?

3 Compare these examples with your own comments in Activity 3A. Are there any similarities between your learning and young children's learning?

Activity 3C

OBSERVING LEARNING

Time 45 minutes

PREPARATION

Group members will need to be asked *in advance* to take ten minutes to observe a child (or small group of children) exploring a new piece of equipment or having a new experience, and to make jotted notes of what they see. The notes would include:

What the child does
What the child says
Other forms of communication (smiles, gestures etc.)

ACTIVITY

1 Working in groups of three or four, discuss your jotted observation notes, telling each other all the important details of the activity you observed. When you all have a fairly clear picture of each other's observations, spend some time talking about these questions:

What seemed to be the most important parts of the experience for the child(ren)?   Why?
Would an adult have responded in the same kind of way? Why? Why not?

2 Think about your methods of observation. Are there improvements you could make?

Activity 3D

BLOCKBUSTER   Time 60 minutes + 45 minutes

PREPARATION

Pencils and paper. Access to a tape recorder, if possible, for the follow up activity.

ACTIVITY   (60 minutes)

1 Working in pairs, imagine you are working with a group of children who are building with bricks and blocks. Make a list of all the possible learning that might be going on. Next, try to think of some questions and comments that might help children to think and talk about what they are learning through their play.

   For example: I see you've made a tiny door in this wall.
                       Can you explain to Sharon why you think that wall collapsed?
                       Has Sharon got other ideas?
                       What else could you try?
                       That part there looks like a castle to me.

2 Working in fours or sixes, compare your list with your colleagues' lists. Do you agree on what the children might be learning? Do you agree on ways of helping them talk about what they are learning?

FOLLOW UP   (45 minutes)

1 During the next few days either make a short tape recording of yourself and some children during a block-building activity; or, if you don't have access to a tape recorder, make some notes on what the children say, and what you say to them.

2 Listen to the tape later, and make some jotted notes of what you and the children say to each other: bring these notes to discuss with your colleagues.

3 Working in the same groups of four or six, look for evidence of children talking about what they are learning. Does their talk give you some insight into what they were thinking about as they played? How would you build on this, next time you join in blockplay with these children?

Activity 3E

SIX INTO ONE WON'T GO

Time   A 30 minutes
       B 45 minutes

PREPARATION

Pencils and paper for A. Copies of *What do we know about learning?* for each group member. For B copies of the '*Learning is* ....'handout. The two parts of the activity are probably best done at different sessions.

ACTIVITY

(30 minutes)

A 1   Working on your own, look over the six statements about learning, and make some notes of examples that illustrate - or contradict - each statement. Use examples from your own experience as a learner, both now and in the past, and examples of children learning in your workplace.

   2   Working in small groups of four or five, discuss each of the statements and the ex-amples you have noted with your colleagues. Think about the implications of each statement for your practice, and your workplace.

HANDOUT 3E

What do we know about learning?

1 Learning is never complete
Even as adults, our understanding continues to develop as we test our new ideas against previous knowledge. Old ideas can be changed in the light of new experiences.

2 Learning is individual
Even if a whole group of children - or adults - are exposed to the same experience, the learning that takes place will be different for each individual. This is because each individual, child or adult, brings to every situation a unique blend of previous experience.

3 Learning is a social event
Some learning takes place in a group. Sharing learning with others can be stimulating.

4 Learning can be enjoyable
This is something that many adults seriously doubt, when they think back to their own schooling. How-ever, learning can be hard, and enjoyable at the same time. Even making mistakes can be part of the fun - how many times did you fall off when you learned to ride a bike?

5 Learning is active
Someone else can teach us, but no one else can do our learning for us. Learning requires our active en-gagement, in doing and talking.

6 Learning means change
The Chinese written character for change is a combination of the characters for pain and opportunity. That sums it up neatly. Sometimes the pain seems to outweigh the promise of new opportunities. As adults we are responsible for keeping the balance manageable for individual children. For us, too, learn-ing may mean painful changes. Sometimes we need to let go of deeply held convictions. The chal-lenge of change through learning may be experienced as exhilarating or as daunting. Often it is both.

B   Principles into practice   (45 minutes)
     Working in the same groups of four or five, select one of the six statements and discuss
     how its message might be incorporated into your workplace, using this format:

HANDOUT 3E
LEARNING IS   write the statement
                                                             you are discussing in
                                                             here

If this is so, then we must
always ...

sometimes ....

never ....

Fill the sheet with your ideas about what should and should not be done to translate this
principle into practice. Try to be as specific and detailed as possible, avoiding vague generali-
sations. Don't shy away from concrete nouns (e.g. dressing up clothes, fire engines, time to talk);
they are much easier to put into practice than fine-sounding abstractions (e.g. opportunities
for development; stimulating environment; language development).

IN WORKING THROUGH THIS SECTION YOU WILL HAVE

REVIEW

considered how what you know about your own learning
can help you promote children's learning

discussed a range of examples of learning by adults and
children, and used these to establish some general
principles

worked on the difficult task of translating principles into
practice

24

Section 4
WHAT DO WE MEAN BY CURRICULUM?

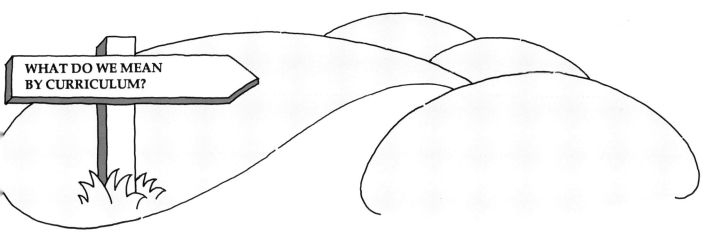

**WHAT DO WE MEAN
BY CURRICULUM?**

IN WORKING THROUGH THIS SECTION YOU WILL BE ABLE TO

- discuss what we mean by a curriculum for young children

- consider what experiences and activities go to make up the curriculum in your own workplace

- talk about the concept of the 'hidden curriculum'

- compare your perceptions of the curriculum you offer with those of your colleagues, and those of the parents of the children in your care.

USERS' COMMENTS

'We realised how little we knew about the curriculum'

'It was interesting to see differences and similarities between the views of parents and workers'

'These activities helped us identify children we should have made greater efforts with'

'This section generated a lot of discussion - and it highlighted the different perspective of special education workers'

WHAT IS IT?

Although we may not use the word curriculum very often, if at all, in our casual conversation, we know that it is an important idea - and, since the arrival of the Education Reform Act and the National Curriculum, it is an idea that appears nearly every day in the national press, on tv and radio. But what exactly does the word mean? And, when we do use it, what do we use it for? Is it a word that really only applies to secondary schools? Or is it a word that we can use to talk about what happens to children in many different settings? (in a nursery class, in a playgroup, in their homes).

In this pack the word has deliberately been used to refer to the whole set of experiences from which children can learn, which we provide consciously - and unconsciously - in a whole variety of settings.

The curriculum for young children includes:

all the activities and experiences provided for them by adults

all the activities they devise for themselves

the language that adults use to them and that they use to each other

all that they see and hear in the environment around them

It is from this curriculum, however planned or unplanned, consistent or inconsistent, that children learn.

WHAT IS IT FOR?

When a curriculum is planned, it will reflect the beliefs of the planners about children, about education, about society. Those who are not part of the planning process may well have very different ideas about what a curriculum should be for. At different times and places, a curriculum for young children has been designed for a wide variety of purposes: some examples are given below; some of them you may agree with, and some of them you may firmly reject.

An early years curriculum may be planned to:

provide a happy, stable and caring environment

provide a stimulating and challenging environment, with opportunities for exploration and discovery

encourage recognition and acceptance of different cultures in a multi-cultural society

prepare young children for school - for adult life - for the workforce

compensate for some deficiencies in the home - physical, social, and educational

instil anti-racist and anti-sexist attitudes

establish patterns of learning for the future

teach accepted norms of behaviour

build on children's experiences in the home by close collaboration with parents.

(These are only a few examples: you may want to add more of your own)

Even a curriculum that has not been planned will have an effect on what young children learn. And it may have a very negative effect; for example:

remove as many objects as possible from the child's reach

punish her if she tries to handle them

punish, scold or ignore her when she asks questions.

Lessons: don't touch, don't ask questions.

Activity 4A

WHAT IS A CURRICULUM MADE OF?

Time 45 minutes

PREPARATION   Make a collection of photographs (from magazines and newspaper supplements or ones you have taken in your own workplace) showing young children in a playgroup, nursery, or infant classroom, indoors and outdoors. Every group member could contribute 5 or 6 photographs. Paper and pencils.

ACTIVITY   1 Share the photographs out, and, working in pairs, make a list of everything in the photographs that is part of the curriculum.

2 Compare lists with other group members.

What have you all included? What have you left out? Discuss the reasons for your agreements and disagreements. Do your lists include space, dirt, noise, other children, adults, fresh air, rabbits, tricycles? Why? Why not?

WHAT IS THE HIDDEN CURRICULUM?

This expression is sometimes used to refer to some un-planned aspects of our provision of which we may be quite unconscious but from which children may nevertheless be learning.

For example, the amount of time and attention that adults give to different activities may suggest to children that some of the things they do are more worthwhile than others.

Some children may receive more attention than others: the children who get less attention may feel that they are less important to the adults. Boys may attract more attention at the expense of girls; or unacceptable behaviour may take up more of our time than behaviour that we approve of and would want to encourage: children may be learning from all of these possibilities. If we frequently praise achievement and the completed product (a jigsaw, or a painting, for example) we may not give enough attention to the effort that has gone into an activity. We may not take an equal interest in all the topics that children intro-duce into discussion: some children may learn that their contributions are not valued. Our provision may reflect our own cultural background, neglecting others; children may learn that things they are familiar with at home (food, toys, songs or stories, for example) are not appreciated, or even acknowledged, away from home.

Activity 4B

THAT'S LOVELY RAYMOND

Time 45 minutes
+ 30-45 minutes

PREPARATION   Copies of the questions below for each group member.

ACTIVITY   The questions below may help you think about one aspect
of the 'hidden curriculum' in your workplace. The way in which we praise or criticise
children may teach them a great deal that we do not necessarily want them to learn.

1 Work in twos or threes to answer these questions, considering what might be the
unintentional effects of your use of praise.

How many children did you praise today/yesterday?
Which children?

What expressions did you use? ('You are a clever boy.'
'What a good girl.') Try to remember your exact words.

What activities were you praising them for? ('You do ride
that scooter well.' 'You did that jigsaw very quickly'. 'What
a beautiful painting.')

What qualities in the children were you praising? ('What a
nice quiet game.' 'You have done that neatly.' Your
castle is quite different from anyone else's.')

NOTE TO GROUP LEADERS

The comments in quotation marks are not offered as
examples of good practice!

2 Now think about the children, the activities and the
qualities that you did not praise. Did you simply ignore
them? Or criticise them? Make a list.

3 Compare your answers to these questions with those of
other group members. What might the children in your
workplace be learning from these patterns of praise and
blame?

(45 minutes)

FOLLOW UP
You might want to ask yourself similar questions about your
use of your own time in your workplace. Which children/
activities take up most of your time? Which receive less of
your attention? What might children be learning from this?

(30-45 minutes)

Activity 4C

WHAT DOES OUR CURRICULUM LOOK LIKE?

Time 45-60 minutes

PREPARATION

Copies of the sentences below for each group member

ACTIVITY

1 Working alone, complete these sentences.

First thing every session....

I let the children....

In our workplace there aren't any....

When I'm planning an activity I always....

The most important aspect of our curriculum is....

Some children in our workplace....

All the children....

I prefer to spend my time....

I try to avoid....

One thing I can't stand is....

I know an activity has gone well....

When I talk to parents about our provision....

At the end of each session....

2 Compare the results with two or three of your colleagues. Do
  you all agree? If not, why not?

FOLLOW UP

You might consider asking some of the parents you work with to complete these or
similar sentences. The differences and similarities in your responses would be well worth
discussing.

In section 7 you will find a range of examples of other approaches to an early years curriculum. You may want to use section 7 as follow-up to your work on section 4. Or if you are taking each section in turn, you may want to keep notes of this discussion to refer back to when you arrive at section 7.

IN WORKING THROUGH THIS SECTION YOU WILL HAVE

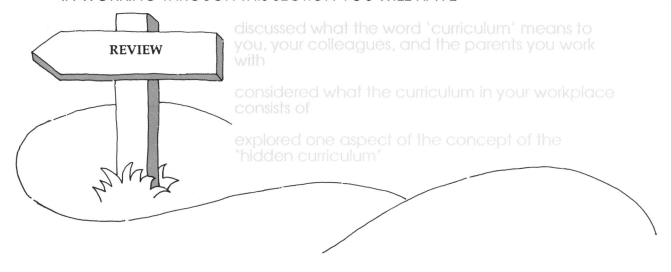

REVIEW

discussed what the word 'curriculum' means to you, your colleagues, and the parents you work with

considered what the curriculum in your workplace consists of

explored one aspect of the concept of the 'hidden curriculum'

Section 5
WHY DO WE DO WHAT WE DO?

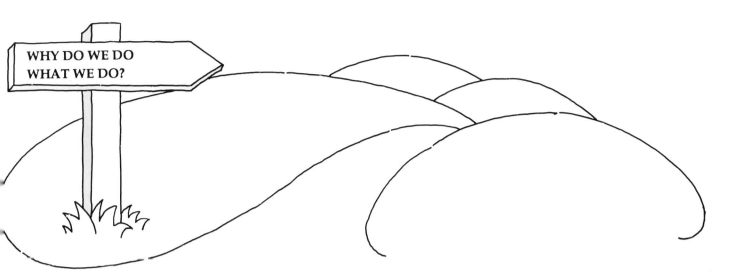

WHY DO WE DO WHAT WE DO?

IN WORKING THROUGH THIS SECTION YOU WILL BE ABLE TO

- think about people and experiences which have influenced your approach to your work with children

- begin to identify these influences in the curriculum you are offering to the children you work with

- think about how you would like to change or develop your approach

USERS' COMMENTS

'This is a very good section to work on with parents'.

'It has helped people to put work with children into perspective'.

'Some of these activities have been a good starting point for generating discussion amongst people who didn't know each other'.

'I hadn't realised how much of what I do was influenced by my own childhood experiences, and how many things have changed since my own training'.

In developing our own curriculum we have all been influenced by many different people and events. Some will be people we know or have known personally, others will have influenced our thinking through their writing. How we behave and react in the workplace is likely to reflect these influences which are changing all the time. How we behave and think is also likely to reflect our values (see section 6).

Activity 5A

WHAT DO WE FEEL IS IMPORTANT FOR LEARNERS?   Time 30-40 minutes

PREPARATION
A copy of the diagram for each group member, or participants will need to draw their own.

NOTE TO GROUP LEADERS
Group members may find it difficult to remember ten separate events from the last week, but this in itself might be a useful starting point.

ACTIVITY
Much of what is put across to children in our care is done implicitly. There are things that we consider important but that are often unquestioned. Sometimes our priorities may relate more closely to our own experiences of childhood than to the lives of children today.

1 Working on your own, think about what skills and experiences you are providing for children. Think of a particular child you work with, and think of the ten most important things that happened to that child in your work place last week. Fill them in on the diagram (below).

```
┌──────────┐      ┌──────────┐      ┌──────────┐
│          │      │          │      │          │
└──────────┘      └──────────┘      └──────────┘
┌──────────┐                        ┌──────────┐
│          │         ╭────────╮     │          │
└──────────┘        (  CHILD'S )    └──────────┘
┌──────────┐        (   NAME   )    ┌──────────┐
│          │         ╰────────╯     │          │
└──────────┘                        └──────────┘
┌──────────┐      ┌──────────┐      ┌──────────┐
│          │      │          │      │          │
└──────────┘      └──────────┘      └──────────┘
```

2 Working in twos and threes discuss your diagrams:

Are these the most important experiences you feel the child should have had?

Would another child have a different list?

If so, why do you think this might be?

Would a girl have a different list from a boy?

Would a black child have a different list from a white child?

Is the list affected by the amount of time a child has been in the group?

Would the child have made the same list as you?

FOLLOW UP
Ask some parents whether they will do this activity, either selecting things that happened to their child at home, or things a parent helper observed in the group.

WHAT DID WE LEARN IN CHILDHOOD?   Time 30-40 minutes

PREPARATION   Paper and pencils.

NOTE TO GROUP LEADERS

This can evoke painful memories for some people and you will need to be sensitive to individual contributions.

ACTIVITY

What are the things that we remember most from our learning?

1   Working on your own, make a list from your own early childhood of 8 - 10 things about your schooling and early experiences that you remember most clearly.

2   Look at your list and try and arrange them in groups. For example, are they about other people, about things, about ways of doing things, about attitudes and values, about your own sex or cultural background, about indoors or outdoors?

3   Working in pairs share and reflect on your lists

4   How do these experiences influence your work with young children?

I'LL NEVER FORGET OLD SO AND SO   Time 45 minutes

PREPARATION   Paper and pencils. The group may like copies of the 'lifelines'.

ACTIVITY

Much of what guides our choice of activities for young children is based upon influences in our life. The influences may be vague and unclear but they can be recognised none the less, if we think about them. This activity will help us consider these influences.

1   Working alone, draw a line. On the left, put the year of your birth; on the right, this year. Divide the line into decades.

Thinking about your own work with young children, roughly mark off those people who had a significant effect on the way that you view your work. A possible line for a teacher might begin to look like this:

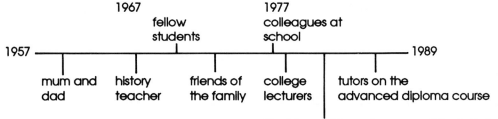

And for a parent helper in a playgroup like this:

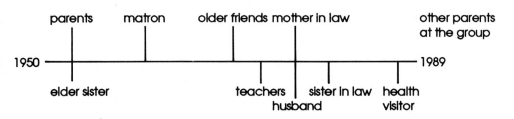

2   Look at your line and consider how much these individuals have affected your thinking and when this occurred.

GREAT NAMES FROM THE PAST

Many early years workers have been influenced (directly and indirectly) by the ideas and values of pioneer educators in Britain and elsewhere. Such names as Froebel, Piaget, the McMillan sisters, Freud, Dewey, Bowlby and Isaacs may be familiar. Tina Bruce's book *Early Childhood Education* (1987) reminds us which basic principles of early years education we owe to these (and other) thinkers.

The next activity is designed to help us think more clearly about such key ideas, and with others in the group, begin to assess their importance to us.

Activity 5D

PRINCIPAL PRINCIPLES?   Time 90 minutes

PREPARATION   A copy of the grid 'Looking at some basic principles' for each group member. Small index-type cards.

ACTIVITY

1 Working alone, each group member should complete the grid.

2 In pairs, compare and contrast your two grids. Try to help each other find out why you differ and agree. Between you negotiate the nine most important statements that you both agree or strongly agree with. Write each separately, on a small card. Look out for contradictions and argue about them! Then arrange the nine cards in a diamond pattern, with the statement your pair thinks is most important at the top......

...and least important at the bottom

3 In the larger group compare your diamond ranking with other people's. Keep asking 'why?' ' But why do you think that is so important?'

FOLLOW UP
If you want to track down the history of the principles you hold to be most important Tina Bruce's book may be helpful. Often we have been influenced by these pioneer thinkers, indirectly, through some of those people we identified in Activity 5C.

LOOKING AT SOME BASIC PRINCIPLES

Please complete this grid individually. Do add any more of your
basic principles in the empty boxes at the end.

Some basic principles of early childhood education*	Strongly agree	Agree	Disagree	Strongly disagree
What children can do (rather than what they can't do) is the starting point in the child's education				
There is an inner structure in the child which includes the imagination and which emerges especially under favourable conditions				
Children learn effectively and efficiently when lessons are highly structured and follow in sequence with a clear progression from task to task				
the people (both adults and children) with whom the child interact are of central importance				
Learning is not compartmentalised, for everything links				
The curriculum should emphasise children as initiators and decision makers, constructing their own knowledge through active learning				
The curriculum should be appropriate to the developmental stage the children have reached				
It is important for adults to reward children's success with praise or other means				
Parents are children's first and main educators in the early years				
Classroom activities need to be carefully matched to the abilities of each child so that no one experiences failure				
Disadvantaged children require a carefully planned and structured environment if they are to succeed				
Children need time and space away from adults so that they can create "worlds of their own"				
Encouraging children to review their own learning is at the heart of effective teaching				

* some of these are from *Early Childhood Education* by Tina Bruce

PRINCIPLES INTO PRACTICE

It's important to clarify our principles, our beliefs and values, because they affect many decisions we make. How we organise our workplace, our time, the resources we have are all influenced by these beliefs.

The next activity involves looking at some evidence from other early childhood workplaces, and talking and thinking about the organisation of these settings. We have chosen to highlight two examples from the 'great names of the past': Maria Montessori and Susan Isaacs. The activity, however, suggests that you collect a variety of other accounts, historical and contemporary, from newspapers and novels, written accounts and visual images.

Activity 5E

OTHER PEOPLE'S CLASSROOMS AND WORKPLACES   Time 75 minutes

PREPARATION

Photocopies of the two extracts for each group member. Ask members to collect examples of other early years workplaces. A good variety might include:

newspapers/magazines; photographs/articles; greetings cards (e.g. painting of 19th Century Dame School); extract from child's or adult books; accounts (such as those overleaf) of a pioneer's work

Each member may need a 'prompt sheet' for this activity:

1 What 'basic principles' underpin this workplace activity?

2 How is it organised?
    children's time
    adults' time
    space
    equipment and resources
    rules
    etc

ACTIVITY

1 In small groups of three or four, examine each of these varied images and accounts. Try to identify the basic principles and organisational structures involved.   (30 minutes)

2 Reflect on how many of the 'basic principles' and organisational structures you have identified in these examples from history, can be recognised in your own work. Which are not present in your work? Why?   (30 minutes)

3 In the larger group share one issue or concern or puzzle that this activity has highlighted about your own practice.
                                                                   (15 minutes)

HANDOUT 5E

In 1907, Maria Montessori was given charge of her first group of normal children, dwellers in a poor district of Rome, and began to experiment with them to see if methods such as Seguin's would be effective on children who were not retarded so much as neglected. It was ten years since she had graduated and begun her work with the mentally subnormal in 1896. By a curious coincidence, Dr Ovide Decroly in Belgium had written in the previous year that he found no differences of nature between normal and abnormal children and that 'the same psychological laws apply - but for the latter, mental development is generally retarded; progress is slowed down, so that in this case one may observe stages which pass so quickly as to be invisible in normal children.'

Long before the opening of the Casa dei Bambini in 1906, Maria Montessori had taught severely-retarded children how to read and write, to the astonishment of the Roman public. She anticipated little difficulty in applying the same principles in the Casa dei Bambini, and in fact encountered none. She introduced Seguin's apparatus for training the senses and, observing that children became absorbed in one item, to the point of repeating an exercise with it forty or fifty times while the next task lay idly by, she began to discard some equipment and form ideas about constructing improved items.

Passing fingers across the letters with his eyes shut, listening to the names of the letters, and tracing them with his index finger and then a pencil, the Montessori pupil linked the sound of the alphabet with touch, sight, and muscular co-ordination. He had to learn how to write before writing. Madame Montessori deduced this from the case of an 'idiot' girl of eleven who could not darn socks or sew a hem. Here Froebel provided a cure, as the teacher remembered his mats in which strips of paper were threaded transversely in and out among vertical strips, providing movements similar to darning. The eleven-year-old, after practice on the Froebel mats, developed her movements for sewing before she encountered the particular problem of sewing; when she returned to it, there remained no difficulty.

From Education Under Six, Denison Deasey, Croom Helm, 1978

'I will describe the school briefly. There is a large schoolroom opening into the garden. At one end of the schoolroom is a platform with a piano, and at the other a rest gallery with mattreses, pillows and rugs. Round the walls, below the window, are shelves and cupboards holding the material which the children use. This is very abundant. There are things for drawing and painting, sewing and modelling, brightly coloured raffia, canvas and wools; the Montessori-material; material for counting, such as counters, beads and shells; an aquarium, a gramophone, books and glasses and bowls for bulbs. Each child has a small table and chair which it can carry about. These have been painted by the children themselves in gay colours. A swing hangs from the gallery.
'Beyond the schoolroom is a cloakroom with bowls for washing, and a gas stove where the children make their own cocoa, and occasionally cook lunch.
'In the garden are an open summer house, a sandpit, a see-saw and hutches for the rabbits. Each child has a plot, and there are fruit trees whose fruit is gathered, cooked and eaten by the children.
'As well as the large schoolroom there are two small rooms where the older children spend part of each morning. Here the more advanced number and reading material is kept, and apparatus, such as dissecting instruments and test-tubes, glass vessels and burners, for scientific observation in zoology, chemistry and physics. A carpenter's bench, a lathe, and a quantity of tools have recently arrived, and one of these rooms will probably become a workshop.

'Leading from these schoolrooms are the children's bedsitting rooms. Each child living in the school has one to himself. These rooms are charming. Each is painted in some bright colour, and each has a gas fire and a settee bed, gay curtains and cushions, and low tables and cupboards. In his own room the child is absolute master. The doors will lock from the inside, and no one is allowed to enter without knocking.

'The school is designed primarily for very young children. All those now coming are between the ages of three and seven, with the exception of one ten-year-old. Several are the children of dons and all are above average in intelligence.

'There is no fixed curriculum. The children do what appeals to them at the moment. The work of the educator is so to select his material, and at times indirectly to suggest activities, that the child will of his own accord do things which are useful for his growth. Lately one or two of the older children have drawn up rough outlines of their day's work. The categories are very wide - for instance, part of the day is devoted to "making things and finding things out" - and their order was arranged by the children themselves after discussion with the Principal. No child would be forced to keep to his programme if he seriously wanted to depart from it at any time.

'The older children voluntarily spend part of each morning at reading and number work. They have reached the stage where they feel the need of reading and writing, and are learning rapidly with no urging. They find the number material interesting and like to use it, though the most valuable part of their number training is probably incidental. A good deal of time is spend in "finding things out" with the help of gas and water, glass vessels and tubes, simple mechanical apparatus, skeletons, and animals alive and dead. A rabbit, crabs, a mouse, and worms have already been dissected. Textbooks will be home-made, in the form of written records of what has been observed.

'The younger children spend a good deal of their time in running about, in conversation, and in simple handiwork. No work involving find hand or eye muscles is encouraged, and no attempt is made to teach them to read. There is, with all the children, much more active movement than one finds in most schools. In fine weather they are out in the garden for most of the day, digging, running, carpentering, or climbing. Even when they are in school the door is often, and the windows always, open. They are encouraged to swing from bars, jump, and supply for themselves in play the kind of exercise which in most schools has been elaborately worked out as drill and gymnastics. The consequence is that their health is excellent. There has been practically no illness since the school began. In two instances people were actually in the school with infectious complaints, which no one caught.

'The aim of the teachers is as far as possible to refrain from teaching, but to let the children find out all they can for themselves. They are urged to answer their own questions, with the teachers to help them discover where the answers are to be found. Above all, care is taken that their ideas of values shall be their own. They are not told that such and such a thing is good or bad, nice or beautiful, but only that it seems so to some particular person.

Evelyn Lawrence on Susan Isaacs' Malting House School

from Susan Isaacs, The First Biography
by D.E.M. Gardner, 1969, Methuen
Educational pp 61 - 65

Activity 5F

FLEXIBILITY AND CHANGE   Time 60 minutes

PREPARATION
Paper and pencils. Copies of the list of questions for each group member.

ACTIVITY
If what we offer to young children is to be relevant to their lives today and in the future, it must be flexible and adapt to meet the needs of the changing society. By noting these changes and the reasons for them we can go some way towards illustrating the source of our viewpoints on the curriculum.

1   Working individually list 10 things that you have tried to develop or change in your work with children since you started working, or since you became a parent.

2   Look back at the list and try to identify what, or who, influenced those changes.

3   Now complete the sentences on the following page.

4   Discuss your answers in the group. Identify the main ways in which you have all had to rethink the way you work with young children and families.

FOLLOW UP
You may find the notes you make on this activity useful in Activity 6E.

IN WORKING THROUGH THIS SECTION YOU WILL HAVE

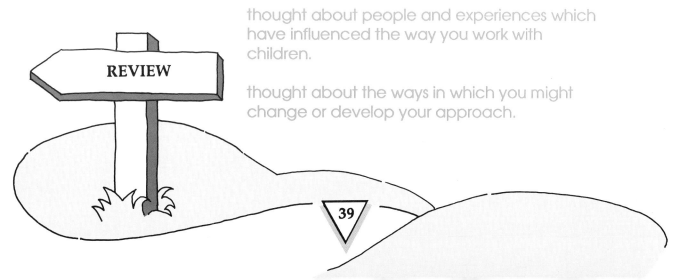

REVIEW

thought about people and experiences which have influenced the way you work with children.

thought about the ways in which you might change or develop your approach.

39

The one thing I would most like to change about the way I work with children is...

I wish could spend more time on...

I would only change my way of interacting with children if...

The main difference between learning in the world when I was a child and learning today is...

When I started working with children I used to think...

Living in a multi-cultural society means...

Working with children whose backgrounds are different from my own has made me think about...

Working with parents has taught me...

Being a parent has taught me...

I am still really worried about...

This is because...

Section 6
WHAT DO WE BELIEVE IN?

WHAT DO WE BELIEVE IN?

IN WORKING THROUGH THIS SECTION YOU WILL BE ABLE TO

- consider how your personal values affect your work with children

- think about how you acquired the values you hold today

- compare your attitudes and values with those of others doing similar work

- look for differences between the values held by different members of your group

- discuss how young children acquire values, inside and outside the home

- look more deeply into *why* you hold certain values

- consider what happens when values are in conflict

- discuss how you and your colleagues make decisions about difficult and controversial issues

USERS' COMMENTS

'This was a very challenging section, but one that we learned a lot from'

'We realised how seldom we thought about our values and how much they influence all that we do'

'Some of these activities were easier in groups where people knew each other already'

'It is difficult to discuss values when most people are adamant they are right!'

LOOKING AT VALUES

'We hold these truths to be self-evident ...' The American Declaration of Independence begins with a stirring summary of the basic principles held in common by its authors. In everyday life, we very rarely openly declare our own 'self-evident' truths. If we are working in a group of adults with shared interests and concerns, we tend to assume, sometimes quite mistakenly, that we all share common, taken-for-granted values.

However, if adults working together have different concerns or conflicting interests, people sometimes begin to question each other about their basic assumptions. These questions may come as a surprise, or be felt as threatening, but sometimes they can be productive in helping us to look more closely at our own values, to consider how and when we acquired them, and to become more skilful at explaining and justifying them to each other.

VALUES IN ACTION

This section of the pack is based on one belief held in common by its authors: that in our work with young children we are affected by our values and attitudes to a host of subjects - we are influenced by our views about, for example, politeness, toilet-training, fighting, dirt, noise, laughter, crying, gentleness, our own parents and our own teachers. Since we ourselves were tiny babies, we have been acquiring values of this kind, often unconsciously, rejecting some of what our peers and parents teach us, and accepting much more. We express these values in our work, not explicitly for the most part, but implicitly, in the thousands of judgements and decisions that we make in the course of a single day. The process of looking inside our own heads and hearts, to find out more about our beliefs and values, is not an easy one. But it can help us to understand more about our own actions, at home and in the workplace.

NOTE TO GROUP LEADERS

This is not one of the easier sections of the pack. Some people may find it very challenging. The experience of opening up and talking about deeply held, but rarely expressed, inner beliefs and values can be a painful one. The suggested activities will probably be most productive once your group has established an easy working relationship, in which every member of the group feels safe enough to express personal points of view. Disagreements between members of the group will, if they can be handled constructively, be of particular importance in work on this section, since it is often through being in opposition to others that we come most clearly to understand what it is we ourselves believe.

Activity 6A

MY MOTHER SAID, I NEVER SHOULD ...

Time   No more than
20 minutes

1   Working on your own, think back to your own childhood. Recall two or three phrases that seemed always to be ringing in your ears from your mother, father, teacher, next-door neighbour, grandmother ...

What were they trying to tell you? What values were they expressing - about your friends, your games, your toys? For example, were you allowed comics? Which ones? Why?

How did you react to what the adults were telling you? Did you obey? resist? rebel?

2   Working in pairs, discuss your thoughts about your childhood. How do you feel now about these experiences? Have you ever caught yourself saying or doing something just as your mother would have done? Or do you deliberately leave the top off the toothpaste?

How much of what you learned in this way are you now passing on, in turn, to the children in your workplace?

Activity 6B

Time 60 minutes

RULES AND REGULATIONS

PREPARATION   Paper and pencils, flip chart/large piece of paper.

ACTIVITY   1   Working in pairs, make a list of all the rules and regulations that you enforce: first, at home, and secondly, in the workplace.
How absolutely do you hold these rules? Are they fixed, and unchangeable? Or do you allow exceptions? When and why? If the rules get bent, who does the bending? What might children learn from these exceptions?

2   Think about how you arrived at these rules. Are they the ones that you remember from your own childhood? Did you, so to speak, inherit them, from your parents and teachers? What values might the children in your care be acquiring as a result?
When you were young, did you obey rules? What did you learn from the rules that were enforced on you? What happened when you were disobedient? Has this affected your attitude to rules today? What about the children in your workplace?

3   In the whole group, consider how what we think is appropriate for children has changed over history. In past centuries in England, parents would take children to watch a public execution. Would you? Would you let a child watch a baby being born? Would you take a child to join a vigil as a close family member died? Would you take a child to a funeral? Would you quarrel with your partner in front of a child? Would you hug your partner in front of a child? ... As you discuss these questions look for points of disagreement, as well as agreement. Think about why you disagree with each other.

43

Activity 6C

IMAGES OF CHILDHOOD   Time 30-45 minutes

PREPARATION | Ask group members to make a collection of pictures of young children, in this country today, in other societies, from the recent and distant past, from newspapers, magazines or your family album ...

ACTIVITY

1 Divide out the pictures and, working in groups of about three or four, consider what these pictures have to say about being a child. What does society here and else-where think children should do and be? Do you all agree?

2 Spend a few minutes looking at each small group's pile of pictures.

3 Working as a whole group, consider how our opinions today have changed - from those of our parents or great grandparents. We no longer expect young children to be part of the work-force - but perhaps our great grand-children will find some of our expectations equally outra-geous ... What do you think?

Activity 6D

FINDING OUT WHERE YOU STAND   Time 30-45 minutes depending
                                                                            on number of statements
PREPARATION
Copies of the 10 statements for each member of the group. This activity works best in a group of 10-12 people.

NOTE TO GROUP LEADERS
Some group members may feel anxious or shy about the physical activity of standing in line: it may be necessary to reassure them that this is a worthwhile and very simple way of getting a picture of the differences between peoples' beliefs. In fact standing in a line as a way of showing what you think is in some ways easier than having to express it in words.

ACTIVITY

1 Working on your own, read the statements and give each one a mark between 1 and 10 to show to what extent you agree or disagree with it. Use 10 for the statements you most strongly agree with and 1 for the statements with which you strongly disagree.

2 Working as a group, take each statement in turn and arrange yourselves across the room in a line that shows the range of opinions expressed. People who strongly agree will be on one side of the room, and people who strongly disagree will stand as far away as they can go. Other people will arrange themselves in order inbetween.

3 When you have made a line for a particular statement, spend some time talking about why people have placed themselves at each point on the line: this is a chance to look at the reasons behind your beliefs and values.

4 Repeat the whole process for another statement: after a while, you will be able to see the wide range of values and attitudes represented in the group. You will also be able to discuss how these values will affect the children in your care.

HANDOUT 6 D
FINDING OUT WHERE YOU STAND

MARKS 1-10

1	Adults make the rules and young children should obey them.

2	When we become parents we often treat our children the way our parents treated us.

3	Boys and girls are born different, therefore they will behave differently.

4	Black British people do not get a fair chance.

5	Children should be looked after at home for the first three years of their life.

6	Children should not be allowed to play with guns and other war toys.

7	Women and girls are unfairly treated in our society.

8	Television is the most damaging influence on young children's development.

9	Children in single parent families are deprived.

10	We live in an unfair, unequal society.

10 = strongly agree
1 = strongly disagree

VALUES, FLEXIBILITY AND CHANGE

During the preceding activities, it may have become clear how the values we hold are not always fixed and static. Rather, they are flexible and dynamic, as we adapt our attitudes to cope with the demands of a changing society. But this process of adaptation is not always an easy one. Faced with changes in the world around us that we find regrettable or deplorable, we may sometimes try to hold on to values that are no longer appropriate, resisting pressures for change and development. Sometimes, it may only be changes that are forced upon us in the workplace that enable us to re-examine long-held and cherished values.

Activity 6E

HOW HAVE I CHANGED?   Time 45-60 minutes

PREPARATION
Paper and pencils. Copies of the list of 'Changes in society'. Notes from Activity 5F if you have done it.

NOTE TO GROUP LEADERS
However long you allow for this activity, it will certainly not be long enough to explore fully all the implications for young children of recent changes in attitudes to cultural background, class and gender. In addition, you may find that some of your colleagues will not willingly accept the need to look critically at their responses to our changing society. You may need to return to these issues more than once in other sections of the pack (for example, activities 4B and 4C). Strong feelings may be expressed and there may be a tendency to take up extreme and apparently unassailable positions. This is inevitable when discussing controversial issues. Don't panic.

ACTIVITY
1 Working individually, look at the list of "changes in society" below and consider how each has affected your work with young children. Add any other important changes that you would like to discuss with the group.

You may find it helpful to record your responses in columns, like this:

CHANGE (e.g. Technology)	MY PERSONAL RESPONSE (your gut reaction - the way you feel about this in your heart of hearts)	MY WORKPLACE RESPONSE (what you do differently at work as a result of this change)

CHANGES IN SOCIETY
1   Attitudes to women working outside the home
2   Greater emphasis on 'back to basics' in education
3   A greater awareness of the multi-cultural nature of society
4   Impact of technology (e.g. television, micro-computers)
5   The outside environment (pollution, safety etc.)
6   etc......

2 Working in groups of three or four, consider similarities and differences in your responses, particularly in relation to, your behaviour in the workplace. Discuss how your changing values might affect the children in your care, thinking particularly about what they are learning from you about themselves, about society and about their care-givers. If you have done Activity 5F, look back over your notes, and discuss similarities and differences.

Activity 6F

PROFESSIONAL OR PERSONAL?   Time 45-60 minutes

PREPARATION   Paper and pencils. Copies of questions 1-5 for each group
                           member.

ACTIVITY   The relationships we form with the children we work with
                           are, in important ways, different from the relationships we
                           form within our family networks. Thinking about these
                           differences may help us understand some of the values
                           that determine our behaviour in various settings.

                    1   Working in twos or threes with questions 1-5 below,
                           consider how you would respond, first, in your
                           workplace, and secondly, at home with your own
                           child(ren), with nieces, nephews, cousins, next-door
                           neighbours etc.

A four year old who is cross with you calls you a 'fat old bum' or a 'silly
old fart'.
What do you feel? What do you say? do?

A three year old viciously bites a younger child in your presence.
What do you feel? What do you say? do?

You discover a boy and a girl (five year olds) in the toilet giggling
about each other's genitals.
What do you feel? What do you say? do?

A five year old says to you 'I think black people stink'.
What do you feel? say? do?

While shopping with a two year old, you momentarily turn your back.
When you turn round, the child has disappeared.
What do you feel? say? do?

Think about why you respond differently in different situations, inside and outside the
home and workplace.

Please add any other incidents from your own experience that you feel would be
worth discussing with the group.

2 Finish the session by sharing your thinking in the whole group

Activity 6G

WHAT *IS* GOOD PRACTICE?   Time 90 minutes
                                                                 (perhaps in 2 sessions)

PREPARATION (by the whole group)
Make a collection of nine extracts from accounts of care and education of young
children, both fact and fiction, using biographies, autobiographies, children's fiction,
to be used for a diamond-ranking exercise. You may wish to re-use materials you
collected for Activity 5E.

NOTE FOR GROUP LEADERS
It is very easy for this discussion to get stuck on the issue of what is 'good' and 'bad',
instead of moving into the much more challenging area of *why* a particular practice
is 'good' or 'bad'. Group members may need a good deal of support and
encouragement from you if they are to make the most of this opportunity to look at
the taken-for-granted reasons that underly their professional judgements.

ACTIVITY
1   Working in pairs, arrange the 9 extracts in this diamond pattern giving position 1 to
    the text that seems to you to come closest to your own beliefs about the best ways
    of treating young children, and position 9 to the one that is furthest away.

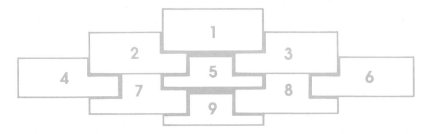

2   Join with another pair to share and explain your choices. Make a list of the reasons
    you give for rating a particular practice as 'good' or 'bad'. This list can now be used
    to explore your values more closely. Taking each reason on the list, consider why you
    have given this justification. For example, you may have decided that one particular
    extract is 'good practice' because it shows children developing self-confidence.
    Now you can consider:' *Why* do I think that developing self-confidence is 'good'?'

3   The session should end with the whole group coming together to discuss their reasons.
    By repeatedly asking yourself and your colleagues 'But why?' (rather like a persistent
    three year old) it is possible, though not at all easy, to come close to the core of your
    own value systems.

Activity 6H

MAKING DIFFICULT DECISIONS

Time 30 minutes
per case study

PREPARATION   Copies of the case studies for the group members

ACTIVITY   As you have worked through this section you will have
                     discovered the wide range of attitudes and values held by
                     the people you work with. You will also have seen how
                     these attitudes and values affect your work. There are
                     often difficult decisions to make in our work, and during
                     this decision making process differences in attitudes and
                     values may become more apparent.

1   Working in groups of four to six, select one or two of the
     short case studies and consider how you as a group would
     decide what to do in each situation.

2   Think about how you, *as a group*, arrived at some kind of
     agreement on what to do. How did people express their
     opinions? Did you use argument? or assertion? How did
     you handle disagreement?

HANDOUT 6 H

1 Parents have been complaining that their children have been coming home swearing. They want the staff to say how they are going to tackle this problem.

2 A child has just been admitted who speaks no English but speaks Cantonese fluently at home. The child's parents are concerned that she should learn English and want only English used in the group. The staff understand the importance of developing the child's home language and want to offer bilingual support.

3 It is the start of the morning session. There are two members of staff on duty, one working in the room, the other supervising some activities out of doors. The member of staff working indoors has carefully prepared a cooking activity which the children have looked forward to, and are waiting to begin. In walks a parent and child (30 minutes late). The parent apologises for being late and it is clear to the member of staff about to begin the cooking activity that the parent is severely distressed. In other words both the parent and the group of children need the member of staff's attention.

4 There is one full day place vacant in a nursery. No other places are likely to become vacant during the next three months or so. The place must be given to one of the following three children (they are the same age). You have this information about them.

(a) a child with Down's syndrome whose parents are in their mid forties. The child's father has a very demanding job and is away from home quite a lot. The child's mother has not been very well and has been finding it difficult to cope as the child grows older and becomes more energetic. The health visitor believes the child would benefit greatly from placement in a nursery.

(b) a child who has recently arrived from Bangladesh (with her mother and two brothers) to join her father who has lived and worked in England for many years. The council are unable to provide a suitable house or flat and the family have been placed in bed and breakfast accommodation. The child speaks no English and is spending all day in a very small room. The health visitor is concerned about the child's welfare and feels that a nursery place would make an enormous difference.

(c) a child from a one parent family. The child's mother is only 18 years old and is finding the responsibility of parenthood overwhelming. The health visitor is concerned because the child looks under nourished and is often dirty. It is clear that both the mother and the child need help and support and it is felt that the nursery could provide this.

Activity 6I

VALUES IN CONFLICT   Time 45 minutes

PREPARATION   Paper and pencils

ACTIVITY

1   Working individually, make a few notes about an incident
    when you came up against someone who seemed to hold
    very different values from your own - away from the
    workplace. Compare notes with two or three of your
    colleagues. How did these incidents arise? How were they
    resolved? How did you feel? How did the other people
    feel?   (15 minutes)

2   Working in the same small group, discuss any similar experi-
    ences in your work-place. What happened? to you and
    to your colleagues? How easy is it to explain and justify the
    values we hold most strongly? Is it easier with someone we
    know well? or with a total stranger?   (15 minutes)

3   Working in the full group, use the ideas you have already
    discussed to consider whether some controversial issues
    are harder to discuss than others. Why? Are disagree-
    ments about racism and sexism, for example, more difficult
    to handle than an argument about nuclear missiles?
    Where do educational disagreements fit in? Can you think
    of an incident when you had a serious disagreement
    about your work with a colleague that you weren't able to
    resolve? What was the effect on you both?   (15 minutes)

IN WORKING THROUGH THIS SECTION YOU WILL HAVE

examined some of your own values that may
affect your work with young children

considered how, when and why you acquired
these values

discussed how you apply these values in your
work with young children

looked for examples of difference and
disagreement as a way of clarifying your own
value position

Section 7
APPROACHES TO THE CURRICULUM

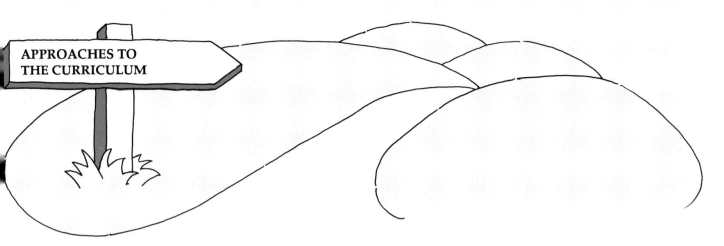

IN WORKING THROUGH THIS SECTION YOU WILL BE ABLE TO

identify key features of your own approach to the curriculum

consider some other available approaches and see whether you:-

can identify any aspects of these approaches in your own

would want to include parts of these approaches in your own

would want to start using one of these approaches

look at local and national curriculum guidelines

USERS' COMMENTS

'There is a lot of good material in this section, but we found some of it very challenging!

'This section really got everyone talking - it was the best fun we had on the course!

'We took a long time over this section, and it really helped us think critically about our own work'

In section 5 you were asked to consider your own approach to the curriculum and to identify people and experiences which had influenced you. Activities 7A and 7B will provide you with an opportunity to consider the children's experience of the curriculum you are offering. If you have done activity 4C, you may find the notes you made useful in preparing for 7A and 7B.

Activity 7A

A CHILD'S EYE VIEW

Time 45-60 minutes

PREPARATION
Before the group discussion in this activity, each participant should observe and keep a diary of how a particular child spends a day or half a day.

NOTE TO GROUP LEADERS
If group members are working in very different settings there may be a tendancy to get bogged down in unimportant details. Members may need encouragement to concentrate on questions of WHY and HOW?

ACTIVITY

1 Working in pairs, discuss your observations of how a child responds to the curriculum you are offering.
What have you learned about
>   the child?
>   your curriculum?
>   yourself?

2 Think about the whole session from the child's point of view:

> the learning environment in and out of doors, including organisation of space and resources
> the daily routine and activities
> interactions with adults

3 In groups of three to four, ask

> *what provision* do you make in each of those areas?
> what choices are available?
> what choices did the child make?
> to what extent did the adults influence decisions?
> what were the child's experiences of different size groups?
> how was the time divided between different activities?
> *why* do you do or provide the things that you do?
> *what* do you hope the children will learn or achieve?
> *how* do you know the children are learning or achieving?
> i.e. how do you evaluate what you are offering the children?
> *which* aspects of your approach are you most/ least satisfied with?

Activity 7B

WHAT'S RELEVANT TO ME?

Time As long
as you like

PREPARATION

Distribute copies of the five examples of different curriculum approaches to each group member before coming to-gether to discuss them.

NOTE TO GROUP LEADERS

The five different approaches are given as examples, not as models which offer all the answers. Group members should be encouraged to look at them constructively but critically.

ACTIVITY

Look critically at the five examples of particular approaches given on the next few pages and ask:-

1 What seem to be the main features of each approach?

2 Would you want to include parts of any of these approaches in your own curriculum?

3 What would you not want to include? Say why.

FIVE APPROACHES TO THE CURRICULUM

1. HIGH/SCOPE

The High/Scope approach encourages children to be problem solvers, decision makers and to be independent. It is a framework, not a rigid programme of activities. It has much in common with good nursery practice but it has a special emphasis on giving children responsibility for planning their own activities.

Set out below is an indication of how adults and children might spend a session in an environment using the High/Scope approach.

It is a practical account of the approach which incorporates arranging the environment to optimise children's learning, using key experiences to observe and plan for the individual needs of children, adult - child communication strategies, partnership with parents, observation and record keeping and so on. It is inevitably schematic and does not show the underlying philosophy, nor how adults can change their practice to encourage children to solve problems, plan ahead, be independent and make decisions.

WHAT CHILDREN AND ADULTS DO THROUGHOUT THE DAY

GREETING
Each child
> comes in and is welcomed;
> hangs up their coat etc. on their peg and leaves articles from home in their storage tub.

Parent and child communicate important experiences and events with workers.

Each adult
> greets parents and children;
> involves them when they are ready.

PLANNING TIME
Each child
> sits on the floor or at a low table with an adult and a small group of children, and parents where possible;
> indicates what he/she is going to do during work time, by for instance:
>> fetching something they want to play with;
>> pointing to an area;
>> naming an area, object, or child he/she is going to work with;
>> describing what he/she is going to do;
>> describing how he/she is going to do something;
>> drawing or tracing what he/she is going to do;
>> dictating or writing what he/she is going to do;
> goes to the area he/she intends to work in as soon as he/she has talked to an adult about his/her plan without waiting.

Each adult
> sits with a small group of children at their level;
> talks individually with each child in turn, asking the child what he/she would like to do, giving the child time to respond, acknowledging the choice or plan the child does make, helping the child expand his/her plan, giving suggestions if the child can't think of anything, reminding the child of something he/she began yesterday, if such is the case;
> watches to see which children need assistance getting started on their plans;
> goes to children who need assistance as soon as every child in the small group has planned.

WORK TIME
(Child initiated and the longest and most important period)
       Each child
           is actively involved with materials he/she has chosen to work with;
           gets his/her own materials from accessible, clearly labelled shelves;
           works on his/her plan or changes the plan if they so wish;
           converses, off and on, with an adult or other children about what he/she is doing;
           attempts to solve problems he/she encounters or seeks the assistance of an adult or another child;
           cleans up his/her own materials when finished with them, unless another child is using them.
       Each adult
           assists children who:
                need help getting started on their plans;
                ask for help as they are working;
                don't seem to know what to do next;
                are making new plans;
           works with children on their own level;
           talks conversationally with children about what they are doing;
           asks open-ended questions to help children extend their plans or solve problems;
           helps children resolve conflict;
           makes sure that children know in good time that the session is about to end.

CLEAN UP TIME
       Each child
           puts materials back where they belong.
       Each adult
           helps children define what materials they're going to put away;
           talks with children about the kinds of things they're putting away;
           makes clean up time fun.

RECALL TIME
       Each child
           sits on the floor or at a low table with an adult and a small group of children (same group as at planning time;)
       Some of the children indicate what he/she did during work time in ways that might include:
           naming the area, object or child he/she worked with;
           describing what he/she did and how he/she did it;
           pantomiming work time activity;
           showing a product made at work time;
           tracing an object used at work time;
           drawing or painting a picture of work time activity or object used.
       Each adult
           sits with a small group of children at their level;
           talks with children:
                asking what they did;
                giving suggestions;
                giving children time to respond;
                acknowledging each child's activity;
                providing language to help each child describe the activity;
                helping children think through problems that came up;
                helping other children to be involved with the child's recall.

CIRCLE TIME
       Each child
           joins the large group activity after finishing his/her small group time activity;
           actively participates in the group game, song, dance, story or planning for special event;
           contributes his/her ideas to the activity at appropriate times.
       Each adult
           leads or participates in the group activity;
           asks children for their suggestions of the activity;
           changes the activity when the children have lost interest.

SMALL GROUP TIME
(Adult initiated but still involving child-choice).
Each child
works with his/her own set of materials;
talks with the adult and the other children about what he/she is going;
helps clean up at the end of the activity.

Each adult
moves from child to child seeing what each child is doing and talking with him/her about it;
asks open-ended questions to help children see new possibilities;
responds to and acknowledges children's efforts and suggestions;
chooses the material, key experience focus for small-group time;
plans a beginning, middle, end;
allows children to use the material in ways that they choose;
observes children's abilities.

OUTSIDE TIME
(In some centres children may plan to work outside during work time).
Each child
may be physically active - running, walking, climbing, pushing, pulling, swinging, exploring;
may be involved with large motor equipment or in an active game.

Each adult
actively participates with children;
talks conversationally with children about what they're doing.

END OF SESSION
Each child
dresses themselves to go home.
Each adult
talks to parents as they arrive to pick up their children.

RECORDING
Each adult writes up the anecdotal records on each child.

FURTHER READING

Hohmann M, Banet, B & Weikart D (1979) *Young Children in Action* - Ypsilanti, High/Scope Press.

An introduction to the High/Scope Curriculum, VOLCUF

Sylva K, Smith T & Moore E (1984-5) *Monitoring the High/Scope Training Programme,* VOLCUF

Smith T & Moore E (1987) *One Year On*, VOLCUF

Carol Tomlinson, High/Scope Development Worker

Further information from High/Scope Institute,
c/o Research and Development Section, Barnado's,
Tanners Lane, Barkingside, Ilford, Essex.

2. RUDOLF STEINER

The principles underlying Waldorf education are based on a clearly worked out view of child development; children grow through different stages and the education they are given must be fully appropriate to these stages. But where Piaget was concerned primarily with the child's intellectual development, Steiner was concerned more broadly with all the characteristics of the growing child. Behind the curriculum lies the idea that through understanding the nature of the child, his emerging individuality can come fully to birth. If this process takes place in a creative and balanced way, then the child will grow into adulthood able to take his place creatively and flexibly, in whatever world he finds himself. The curriculum aims to give the child a balanced experience of the arts and sciences, and balance in his processes of thinking, feeling and willing; it seeks to educate more than the intellect alone, giving children open rather than limited options.

The kindergarten, which takes children from the age of 4 until 7, is viewed as a special place, and is often separated off from the rest of the school. From the moment the children begin kindergarten, the teacher attempts to engage the child's whole being in what they do, in as artistic a way as possible, by providing a warm and joyful environment in which the child can feel nurtured and at ease, happy to explore and play, be busy or be still. The teacher provides a pattern for each morning. The day may begin with time together in a circle, with a morning song, singing and circle games, some quiet and gently, others vigorous with plenty of clapping and moving, before the children are guided, sometimes through a story into their play. The children are free to play, draw or sew, with others or alone, with the teacher ready to help or join in. There is no attempt to give the child purely intellectual activities, as these come at a later stage; the children are not given instructional materials to prepare them for reading and number skills for example. Although children certainly can be taught these at very early ages there is no real need to furnish them yet with abstract symbol systems, as they can be learned later at a stage more appropriate in their development. Now is not the time to give the children intellectual achievements but to give them a broad scope for the full play of their imagination, at an age in which the imagination is a wonderful source for play, and a rich basis for activity.

How does the child experience these ideals in a Waldorf curriculum?

The children enter the room and are personally greeted by their teacher. The room is painted and in a warm colour, has few hard rectangular corners, and is often furnished with soft muslins to mark off a different area, or draped over a window to give a softer quality of light. The quality of sound is that of human voices rather than of mechanical toys. The materials in the room are natural and are at the children's level, and stored in aesthetic containers such as simple baskets or wooden boxes which may themselves be incorporated into the play.

There is no lego, nor any pre-formed or pre-scribed games, nor are there plastic toys. Instead there are wooden blocks of every dimension and texture that are made into all manner of things. Imagination plays the central role in the Waldorf kindergarten, with all the simple materials there to be used as the children's play evolves. Baskets of pine cones, shells, pieces of wood and bark, are emptied and the children make a layout that grows as they play and make up their story. Small felt dolls are brought to join in, or simple puppets come to help tell the story, while the younger ones watch on. For in this kind of kindergarten there is often a three year age range, which is welcomed as an important contribution to the play and social experience of the children. There are baskets of wools and fleece and felts ready for little fingers to be helped in making simple purses or balls. A workbench is available with small but real vice and hand drill, hammer and saw where the children can make their own wooden hammer or boat or simple frame loom.

The house corner is furnished with cribs in which are sleeping home-made soft dolls, waiting to be awakened, and there are simple wooden cookers and ironing boards and so on created to have simplicity, look pleasing, and have lots of scope. There is no television through which to view a different world, for there is enough to be busy with in the real world within the kindergarten.

The room that was quiet is filled with the lively sound of children making much out of little, stimulated by the very simplicity of the materials they set out with, free rein given to their imagination. There are clothes horses, and cloths of all sizes and colours, waiting to be seized upon by eager hands and be transformed into whatever kind of structure or situation the children conceive .... horses, dens, rabbit burrows, ships or whatever. Tables and chairs become castles or shops .... Children are called to come and crawl into the foxes den, or climb up into the carriage that's carrying the queen to her wedding, or to join in with whatever is being imagined.

The middle of the morning comes, and it's time for everyone to put everything away and come to the table for a snack. The children sit together around the joined up tables. In the centre of the table there are flowers, or whatever befits the season or the festival, and a candle to be lit. For the daily and weekly rhythm of the kindergarten is set within the wider rhythm of the year, so that the children develop an awareness of the world around them and their own place within it.

The seasons and the festivals give a rich and meaningful basis for songs, games and stories. The snack is simple, maybe bread, which they may have helped to make, with the jam they picked fruit for and stirred in the Autumn, with a drink of juice, served in simple ceramic cups. The children and teacher sing a blessing together before the food rapidly vanishes. Some of the children help to wash up and put away the things, and then it is often time to go out and play.

The outside play equipment is intentionally minimal, with maybe a few swings and a big sand area, but when space allows there are plenty of natural play things .... tree trunks and logs to scramble over to be splendid ships for all to climb on, or to find woodlice under .... bushes to make dens in and slopes to run down .... a small garden to dig and plant bulbs in or tend according to the season. In having little given equipment the children become all the more creative in the play they evolve. And there are other things to do outside, walks to go on, where possible apples and plums to be picked and carried back in baskets ready for jam making, conkers to be found, squirrels to watch, or a stream to paddle in.

The teacher tries throughout the morning to achieve a balance in the activities the children are engaged in. On particular days of the week they do French and German songs and games, baking, hand-work, and eurhythmy, (which is a form of movement), or painting. The paints used are watercolour and the brushes and paper are of good quality. The children learn how to best hold their brush to apply the paint, by painting alongside their teacher, and they paint onto wet paper. Often the teacher begins the painting time with a song, a story or image, for example of the fire coming as they bring in the red. The children have only primary colours and surprise themselves with the colours and forms that arise before their eyes.

The kindergarten teacher has thus an extra important role to play, for if the children are learning for example how to paint, or pick apples or make their hammer, by imitating the way he or she does those things, then they have to be done well; the kindergarten teacher has to be especially worthy of the children's imitation.

As the morning draws to a close the children gather into a special corner of the kindergarten where there are seasonal decorations; in the autumn there may be branches with cones, rocks, and crystals catching the light. A child is asked to light the story candle, and a hush falls as the children wait for their teacher to tell them the story .... tell them it, not read it for in the Waldorf kindergarten it is felt to be important for stories to be told directly to the children rather than with a book placed between them. So the teacher has to be especially well prepared, and be able to kindle within the children their own pictures in their own mind's eye. The children are asked to be continually active inwardly, as their mental world is furnished with images either from the natural world or from a vast store of fairy tales, through which they can travel far and experience much, stories which seek to nourish rather than merely entertain or instruct, and are lasting rather than transitory. And so the morning comes to a close with a farewell song before the children leave.

FURTHER READING

Edmunds, L.F. (1986 - reprint) *Rudolf Steiner Education*, Rudolf Steiner Press.
Harwood, A.C. (1985) *The Recovery of Man in Childhood*, New York: The Anthroposophic Press.
Piening, E and Lyons N (1979) *Educating as an Art* Rudolf Steiner Press.
Rudel, J & S (eds) (1972) *Education Towards Freedom* Lanthorn Press.
Spock, M. (1978) *Teaching as a lively art* Anthroposophic Press.

Judith Woodhead, teacher and parent of children at a Steiner school.

3.   MONTESSORI

Dr. Maria Montessori saw the child as much more than someone who simply had to be entertained in the best way possible for him to learn. She saw the child as the builder of the future. Her idea was that in aiding the child to develop his fullest potential through his own efforts, she was aiding, in a small way, the development of a more peaceful and harmonious world. Her thoughts were not simply confined to the age group for which she is best known in this country, 0 - 6, but spanned life from birth to maturity. As far as child development was concerned, she grouped the ages from 0 - 6, 6 - 12, 12 - 18.

Dr. Montessori observed that children in the $2^1/_2$ - 6 age group seemed to have a different type of mind to that of children there after. This mind seemed capable of absorbing the complexities of life without effort. The child has no choice but to take in what surrounds him - he unconsciously absorbs what he sees, absorbs the world without effort. Let us then provide what good and rich experiences we can to assist in the foundation it would lay for the very being of the child.

The learning environment in and out of doors, including organisations of space and resources.

The child is in the process of refining both his senses and his language. He does not reason or use language as a child of over six. Therefore one cannot use reasoning or language to convey concepts to the child under six as one can in a school environment with an older child. The young child leans through observation, movement and exploration. Emotionally, the child needs security, love and affection, and a protected environment. The child over six can be directed and corrected by language and reasons. For the child under six this approach is inappropriate. So where possible the direction and correction for the young child should be inherent in the structure of the environment. Foundamental to our approach is the belief that (to quote Dr. Montessori) 'the child constructs himself, that he has a teacher within himself and that this inner teacher also follows a programme and a technique of education, and that we adults by acknowledging this unknown teacher may enjoy the privilege and good fortune of becoming its assistants and faithful servants, by helping it with our co-operation.'

The physical elements of the environment include the actual rooms themselves and the outdoor areas accessible to the children. The rooms would be arranged to convey as closely as possible a home for the children and not a school. Areas may be designed for quiet activities, reading, floor activities or table work. Free access where possible should be provided to the garden. This is especially important for children in an urban area. The furniture - chairs, tables, sinks and lavatories should, of course, be childsize.

The shelves on which the materials and activities are displayed should be low enough for the children to easily collect whatever they require, whenever they require it. With the exception of sinks and toilets there is generally only one example of each activity. And each activity will be complete within itself. Everything the child will need for a particular activity should be found in one area. There will be specific places, for instance, for each piece of equipment and specific places where one can find extra supplies to replenish materials used so that when a child returns the activity to the shelf it will be ready in good order for the next child who may want to use it. This intrinsic order allows the children the opportunity to be responsible for their own Children's House.

The daily routine and activities

Marla Montessori called her classes for $2^1/_2$ - 6 year olds 'Children's House'. In these houses children work together in a mixed age group. Ideally there are no fixed work periods and children are able to choose their own work and to repeat any particular activity for as long as they like. The freedom to choose work and to repeat an activity for any length of time are important factors in helping children develop their personality and express their potential. The child is given the freedom to interact with his environment.

Helping children towards acting independently in all areas of their life is one of the most important aspects of the Children's House. By showing the children how to pour their milk, how to tie their laces, how to wipe their nose, greet a person, etc, we are helping them to perfect their physical co-ordination, thereby enabling them to perform skills and techniques which can be applied for themselves and to those around them. Gradually the children become less dependent on adult help. By actively contributing and participating in the adult world, their self esteem grows, they become more confident and self motivated.

The children work individually most of the time, coming together when they wish to at different periods during a day. These periods are not set, but arise out of the needs of the children on that particular day.

They work with materials which are designed from a developmental point of view and which help the child to make successive levels of discovery about his world. So, the emotional or psychological elements include: that the child is free to watch; that the child is free to choose his or her own activities; the child is free to follow his or her own natural rhythm and work pattern; that the child is a key member of the school - it is his or her *own* house; and that the child must feel secure and loved in that home.

The social elements in a Montessori Children's House are equally important and fundamental. Every Montessori class has a MIXED

AGE GROUP. A class should ideally contain children between 2¹/₂ and 6 years of age. A mixed age group gives the child a chance to be among a group of people of extremely disparate talents and abilities. It affords the child the opportunity to help and be helped by people other than adults. The mixed age group gives the child a chance to be a younger and then an older member of an intimate group. It provides infinite opportunities for role playing within a real setting with real activities.

Planning and record keeping - the role of the adult.

How is all this organised into a coherent and enjoyable experience?

The adult has four main tasks. Firstly, to prepare *herself*. She will involve herself in a side by side learning situation with the child. She is fallible. However, she will take direct attitudes when her experience and maturity are required and will not, for example, sit back and watch while a child deliberately harms either another child or the environment.

Secondly, to prepare the environment. By providing a stimulating and challenging environment this will aid the child by creating a spontaneous learning situation.

Thirdly - actively to put the children in touch with their environment through directing their energies. She acts as a link between the child and the materials. She teaches by demonstration and example, not by correction.

Fourthly - observation. She observes each child, notes his or her interest, how he or she works. She then uses these observations to decide what next might be presented to the child, how it should be presented, and when. She must have in mind and be ready to present and help the child to the next stage of development. She must also note how much freedom an individual child can cope with - and support his or her current needs. She is the child's helper. She directs his exploration, as and when he or she needs it. She is not a teacher in the traditional sense - hence the name - Directress.

FURTHER READING

Maria Montessori, *The Absorbent Mind*, Clio Press Ltd.
Maria Montessori, *The Secret of Childhood*, Sangram Books.
Maria Montessori, *The Discovery of the Child*, Clio Press Ltd.
E.M. Standing *Maria Montessori: Her Life and Work*, New American Library.
Mario M. Montessori, *Education for Human Development - Understanding Montessori*.

Further information from The Montessori Society, 26 Lynhurst Gardens, London NW3 5NW tel. 01 435 7874.

4. STRUCTURED, PRE-PLANNED LESSONS

Very often the detailed pre-planned lessons which have been devised by 'experts' and are produced in packs are associated with American programmes. While many such packs are used in the USA it is wrong to believe that these are used exclusively across the Atlantic. Many European and Third World countries use such programmes or packs. The curriculum design is usually devised by educationalists who consider stages of child development and usually base work on particular theories of child development. Maria Montessori is considered by many to come under this heading. Her close observation of children led her to produce guidelines for their development. Bereiter and Englemann are names often associated with this approach though many of us are more familiar with Peabody, or Distar.

This direct instruction method normally has detailed manuals which provide daily, (small) group instructions for staff to use with children. The lessons are highly structured and sequential with each lesson being dependent upon the previous lesson taught.

Elements of this approach are also found in growing numbers of work books and schemes for use with children at home.

This direct instruction method has not gained the widespread acceptance in the United Kingdom that is received in many other countries, but the following examples produced in England from *Teach Them to Speak*, by G M Shiach (1972) is typical of a pre-planned lesson which a teacher could follow.

Daily lesson 97

Materials

1   Tool cards (as below)
2   Nursery rhyme - Monday's child

Procedure
Ask the class what today is called. Ask them to say the names of other days. Then ask them to chant the names of the days of the week. Repeat as often as enthusiasm allows. Vary the pace of the chant, and have the class emphasize the first syllable of each day. Ask several children who are familiar with the order questions like 'What day comes after Tuesday?' and 'What day comes before Thursday?' Ask those who are still confused to chant out the days they are familiar with, in order. Finish by having the class recite Monday's child.

Make the children close their eyes as you describe one of the tools. Have them guess what the object is. Try and avoid mentioning its function in your description although you may need to say where or in what activity the object is used. Ask the child who answers to name the function of the tool. Then display the appropriate picture.

1 knife	2 telephone	3 spade	4 hat	5 soap
6 light bulb	7 pencil	8 bottle	9 tap	10 book
11 clock	12 scissors	13 spoon	14 straw	15 bicycle
16 lawnmower	17 car	18 rubber (eraser)	19 screwdriver	20 needle
21 thread	22 toaster	23 shoe	24 glass	25 letter
26 hammer	27 wheelbarrow	28 hairdryer	29 tin opener	30 pencil sharpener

Have the class follow simple instructions like 'close your eyes and stand on one leg'. Vary the length and difficulty of your instructions according to the level of the class. Repeat as often as the enthusiasm of the class allows. Increase the pace of the instructions as you go along.

5. THE PORTAGE PROJECT

Portage is a structured individualised home-based programme to teach skills to pre-school children with a developmental delay.

It was conceived in Wisconsin, USA and has been adopted by many local authorities in this country. It should be a multi-agency approach involving agencies from health and social service to education and volunteers.

The Portage model involves a weekly home visit to the parent and child by a trained Portage home teacher who is normally supported by a local Portage group on a fortnightly basis.

Teaching activities are negotiated with the parent for the parent to follow and the parent records daily information about the task the child performs. The tasks are based around the parents' concerns and knowledge about their own child. The scheme benefits the parent by offering her regular support from the home teacher, and reinforces the parents ability to work successfully with her own child.

The Portage materials comprise
1. A Portage checklist covering six sections: infant stimulation, socialisation, language, self help, cognitive and motor skills.
The checklists are sequences from 0 - 6 years. They help the parent and home visitor to focus on what skills the child has already achieved and what skills are 'emerging'.
2. Teaching cards which offer practical teaching suggestions and are similarly sequenced to link with the checklists.
3. Activity charts on which to record the activity and give instructions to the parents as to how to teach the activity.

Positive attributes of the scheme are:
a) it reinforces parents' abilities to be parents;
b) work with the child starts with where the child *is* and not where he/she *ought* to be;
c) it is regular support to parents of a child;
d) because each task is broken down into manageable steps , a child can easily achieve and be successful;
e) it can introduce new play materials to the child;
f) it offers the opportunity for workers from different disciplines to work together in a cohesive way with parent and child.

Possible difficulties are
a) parents need to be motivated to maintain and record the activities;
b) home visitors need to be aware of the parents' level of literacy as it usually involves written recording;
c) it may not be a useful model within a 'chaotic' family unit because of its highly structured nature.

A child's reaction to Portage

In the experience of Portage visitors, most children appear to enjoy the programme. It offers a child new toys and materials sometimes not normally available in the home setting. It offers a child a focus to her week and her own special person to work with. Because the tasks are attainable the child achieves and receives positive reinforcement through praises and reward. Within a family where there are other children it means that the 'Portage' child is given a space every day where she receives Mum or Dad's attention. The scheme is for the child and although Mum/Dad may incidentally receive support the benefit and time is primarily for the child.

FURTHER READING
Bluma, S. et al (1976) *The Portage Guide to Early Education* Wisconsin: Co-operative Educational Service Agency
Revill, S & Blunden, R (1980) *A manual for implementing a Portage home training service for developmentally handicapped pre-school children* NFER/NELSON
Weber, S et al (1975) *The Portage Guide to Home Teaching* Wisconsin: CESA.

6. NATIONAL GUIDELINES

In recent years teachers of young children have been on the receiving end of a flood of official documents about the curriculum. One of the more influential has been *The Curriculum from 5 to 16 - Curriculum Matters 2* (HMSO 1985), which formulates broad educational aims for both primary and secondary schools.

In this pamphlet curriculum is seen as something more than a school's formal timetable or programme of lessons. The authors of the pamphlet (members of Her Majesty's Inspectorate) attempt to describe every aspect of children's learning in school - in play-grounds and corridors, as well as in classrooms.

The pamphlet describes two essential and complementary perspectives on curriculum

nine areas of learning and experience

four elements of learning

These two perspectives are shown diagrammatically on the following page.

HANDOUT 7C

This diagram reveals boxes into which a curriculum, or parts of a curriculum, can be theoretically sorted. But what do the abstract phrases that label each box mean in practice? In what ways could we use this analytical framework in planning and reviewing our work with young children?

	4 ELEMENTS OF LEARNING			
9 AREAS OF LEARNING AND EXPERIENCE	KNOWLEDGE (i.e. facts)	CONCEPTS (or ideas)	SKILLS	ATTITUDES
1. AESTHETIC & CREATIVE	1	2	3	4
2. HUMAN & SOCIAL	5	6	7	8
3. LINGUISTIC	9	10	11	12
4. MATHEMATICAL	13	14	15	16
5. MORAL	17	18	19	20
6. PHYSICAL	21	22	23	24
7. SCIENTIFIC	25	26	27	28
8. SPIRITUAL	29	30	31	32
9. TECHNOLOGICAL	33	34	35	36

Activity 7C

CURRICULUM TOMBOLA

Time 30 mins at any
one session

PREPARATION Copies of the diagram for each member of the group and 36 straws, numbered 1-36. One member of the group will need to take notes.

NOTES FOR GROUP LEADERS

This activity needs to be briskly chaired or it can become monotonous. The activity might be most useful if used more than once, for brief periods (for example, 20 minutes at a time at two or three consecutive meetings).

After a few sessions it may become evident that there are particular elements or areas of learning in which group members find it easier or more difficult to find examples of children learning. The group may find it useful to think further about why this is so.

Is it due to the limitations of this particular curriculum framework?

Could it be due to gaps or under - or over-emphasis in provision?

ACTIVITY

1 The numbered straws are shuffled. One group member chooses a straw, and refers to the grid above.

Thinking back over the last few weeks, share with colleagues an experience for an individual child or several children which you believe has led to the element/area of learning identified by the numbered straw. If no example of this type of learning can be found in the last few weeks, then describe an example from past experience, or an imaginary example.

Other members of the group must not disagree with this contribution. Your contribution is to ask penetrating and challenging questions about each contribution; and then to add your own examples of this type of learning. The object of the activity is not to negotiate one agreed meaning, but to listen to and experience the variety of meanings within the group. There can be. therefore, no right or wrong descriptions. The note-taker should record, as briefly as possible, the whole variety of examples.

2 When one box of the grid has been discussed another member of the group selects a straw and the process continues.

▽ 69

7.   CURRICULUM GUIDELINES FROM LOCAL AUTHORITIES

The publication of *Curriculum Matters 2*, the Education Reform Act of 1988, papers from the National Curriculum Council and developments in the social services sector, have led many local authorities to produce written guidelines for services for young children. These are varied in content and it would be impractical to attempt to summarise them. The most useful approach is to look at the guidelines produced in your area and/or for your service and consider some of the questions in Activity 7D.

Activity 7D

EXAMINING LOCAL GUIDELINES

Time 30 - 60 minutes
(or longer,
depending on
guidelines)

PREPARATION
Each member of the group will need to have read the local guidelines. If education and social services departments have produced separate guidelines, it might be worth looking at both.

ACTIVITY

In groups of three and four discuss the questions below.

1.   Do the guidelines have an underlying philosophy? Is this philosophy spelled out or left implicit? In such a philosophy what emerge as the needs of children, of families, of services and of those who provide the services?

     Look back to section 6. Do the values of such a philosophy seem to be consistent with your values?

2.   Do the guidelines appear to have been influenced by any of the major schools of thought on curriculum?

3.   Do the guidelines assume that all children are the same or is there specific recognition of cultural differences?

4.   Do the guidelines talk only of he or of she, or assume gender-related patterns of play or use of play materials?

5.   What is left out? For example, do the guidelines assume a particular age range of children? Of training and/or experience of staff? Do they assume a particular pattern of relationship with parents?

6.   What are the implications of the guidelines for you? If you and your colleagues were responsible for implementing the curriculum in the guidelines what would it mean for you in time, energy, reorganisation, questioning of your assumptions?

IN WORKING THROUGH THIS SECTION YOU WILL HAVE

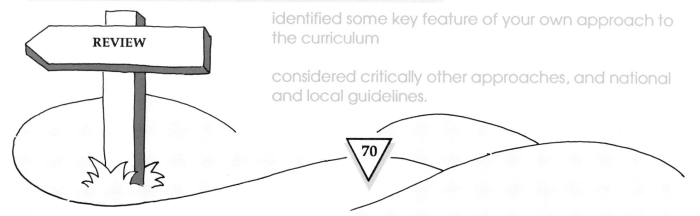

identified some key feature of your own approach to the curriculum

considered critically other approaches, and national and local guidelines.

REVIEW

70

Section 8
OBSERVING CURRENT PRACTICE

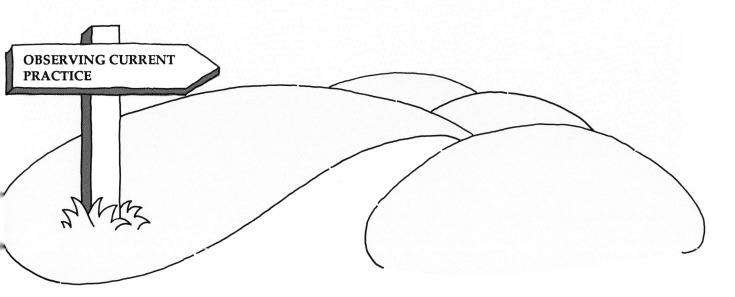

OBSERVING CURRENT
PRACTICE

IN WORKING THROUGH THIS SECTION YOU WILL BE ABLE TO

- discuss the most useful ways of observing for you and your colleagues

- try out some observations in your work place as a way of examining your practice

- think about the use of questions as a framework for observation

- discuss with your colleagues the questions that you want to ask about your practice

- consider how your internal values affect what you choose to observe, and the interpretations you make of your observations

- after making observations, decide what the next most useful step will be

USERS' COMMENTS

'This section was particularly worthwhile - very valuable to our nursery'

'It made us very aware of what is and isn't happening in our nursery'

'A good basis for very lively discussion'

'It made us realise how little we really observed all children'

WHY DO WE NEED TO OBSERVE?

Have you ever had the experience of driving - or cycling - or walking to work, and, on arrival, realising that you have no conscious memory of the journey? You must have taken hundreds of decisions during that journey (faster, slower, stop at the traffic lights, know it's safe to proceed) but you did so without consciously thinking about it: you'd been travelling, in effect, on automatic pilot.

Something of the same kind can happen in our work with young children. We can get so caught up in familiar routines that we no longer respond to the richness of what is going on around us. We cannot possibly respond to everything that happens in a room full of active children and adults, so we concentrate on just one or two aspects of our surroundings - perhaps one child who's worrying us, or a new piece of equipment, or an activity that needs particularly sensitive adult involvement.

Much of the rest of what's happening may be almost invisible to us unless something goes drastically wrong, when our built-in mental radar equipment will quickly send us to the scene of the disaster.

There is nothing wrong with this way of working; indeed, we have had to learn to behave like this to be able to cope with the confusion and complexity of our work. But from time to time, it is worth taking a second look at some of the taken-for-granted everyday experiences that go to make up our current practice. One powerful way of doing this is through observation.

There are as many ways to observe as there are observers; and this pack cannot offer a comprehensive survey of observation techniques. Books that you might find useful on this topic are listed in Section 11. Instead, this section offers you some observation activities that other workers with young children have found useful in the past.

You will be able to decide whether and when to try them out for yourselves,and, more important, how to adapt them to your (and your colleagues') present concerns.

Two of the observation activities (8B & 8C) are based on the principle that framing questions about our practice, and making observations in order to answer those questions, is an effective way to evaluate, and, in due course, improve that practice. Both activities offer you the opportunity to move from description to analysis, to reflection and to action. As you frame questions about your practice, and take steps to answer them, you will, inevitably, be influenced by your own beliefs about what is most important in your work with young children. Once again, the values that you examined in your work on section 6 will be shaping your behaviour. Carrying out the observations may be a useful way of exploring how your inner values affect the way in which you perceive the outer world.

Activity 8A

PREPARING TO OBSERVE

Time 30 minutes

PREPARATION
Paper and pencils

ACTIVITY
Before tackling 8B and 8C, it is useful to try and reach a clearer understanding of what observation involves.

1 Working on your own, think about what the term 'observe' means to you. Write a brief definition.

2 Working in pairs, think about the kinds of things you think it would be useful to observe in your own workplace.

3 Finding time to observe, and just as importantly, to record one's observations, is a challenge faced by most adults working with young children. Consider how you could make observations a more regular part of your work by identifying:
    all the things which make it difficult for you to observe
    all the things you could do to make observation easier.

4 Finally come together as a group to share what you have identified.

Activity 8B

FINDING QUESTIONS OF YOUR OWN

Time 30-45 minutes

PREPARATION
Copies of the incomplete sentences overleaf for each group member.

ACTIVITY
Being told to go out and find questions of your own may feel a bit like being told to go and find the proverbial needle and haystack. Where to begin?

Completing the sentences overleaf might be a useful starting point. First complete them on your own, then work in pairs or small groups sharing your perceptions of strengths and weaknesses. You will then be able to reach a joint decision about what you want to examine in more detail through the use of questions.

I have given *most* thought to the following areas/activities in the workplace ...

I have given *least* thought to the following areas/activities ...

I am *most* pleased about ...

I am *least* pleased about ...

The children seem to use the following areas/activities *most* constructively ...

I think this is because ...

The children seem to use the following areas/activities *least* constructively ...

I think this is because ...

I spend *most* of my time working with children in the following areas/activities ...

I spend *less* of my time working with children in the following areas/activities ...

I would like to spend more time ...

I think I *most* need to look critically at the following areas/activities...

Activity 8C

WHY? WHAT? HOW? WHO?

Time 45-60 minutes

PREPARATION   Copies of the questions below for all group members

ACTIVITY   Once you and your colleagues have identified something
                            you would like to look at in more detail, you could use the
                            framework given below to help you make a plan. If you
                            work in a team, it is most effective if everyone is involved in
                            this process

1 WHY?   Why are you interested? What are your reasons for looking
           at this part of your work?

2 WHAT?   What exactly is it that you want to know? You might be
           interested in some or all of the following:

           organisation of space

           organisation of time

           equipment
           (e.g. children's access to the equipment, its condition, its
           relevance to a multicultural society, gaps in provision etc)

           rules and regulations

           adult involvement

           individual differences and individual needs
           (e.g. immature children, children who need to be
           stretched intellectually)

           the place of spoken language
           (e.g. the needs of children learning English as a second or
           third language, language delayed children, etc.)

3 HOW?   What observation techniques will be most useful in helping
           you? (for example, jotted notes, photographs, tape-
           recordings; see also the books suggested in Section 11
           and particularly *Working with young Children* by Jenny
           Laishley).

4 WHO?   Are there other adults who could usefully be involved in
           the observation process?

The results of joint discussion of these four stages can now be used to frame the specific questions you want to examine.

For example, the questionnaire that follows was devised by the staff of a nursery school in Bristol to help them observe their home corner provision. Answering the questions involved them all in observation. The purpose of the observations was in part,to help them to be critical of their own provision - but the process didn't seem threatening since they remained in control of what they were doing.

OBSERVING THE HOME CORNER

RULES

1 Are there rules?
2 What are these rules?
3 Do all children know these rules?
4 How do they learn the rules?
5 On what basis are the rules made?
6 Who maintains the rules?
7 Are there any rules which could be eliminated?
8 Through observation can you see any new rules which should be made?
9 Do particular children make their own rules which they then enforce on other children?

EQUIPMENT

1 What equipment is available for the children's use in the home corner?
2 What equipment is held in reserve?
3 What other equipment is needed?
4 Is there other equipment in the school which could be used/shared?
5 Which equipment is being used least/most/not at all?
6 Is equipment being used by all or particular children?
7 Are the children using the equipment in the manner in which you would expect or are they putting it to alternative uses?

LANGUAGE

1 What language opportunities do you expect from the equipment provided?
2 Is this language achieved?
3 Could it be extended? If so, how?
4 Does the language change over the week or is it stereotyped?
5 Listen carefully to the language.

CHILDREN

1 Which children are using the home corner?
2 Are the same children using it all the time?
3 Are the children who need the home corner most, making use of it?

ADULTS

1 How much time do you spend in the home corner?
2 How do you see your role in home corner play?

PLAY

1 Are children involved in parallel, associative or co-operative play?
2 Is the play repetitive in nature?
3 Look for make believe play - does it all relate to known situations?
4 Does the play determine the language children are using?

Activity 8D

CURRICULUM IN ACTION

NOTE FOR GROUP LEADERS

Time 6-10 hours
spread over a
number of sessions

This activity is based on materials published by the Open University*, which form a substantial in-service course for teachers, but it can just as easily be applied in other settings. Before embarking on this activity, it would be appropriate to think about ways in which the present group might want to adapt or modify or select from the material presented here.

The original *Curriculum in Action* pack has been used by teachers working in groups in teachers' centres or in their own schools. They usually start by making one or two short observations in their own classrooms, using all six questions. Next, they take each question in turn and use it as the focus for further classroom observation. Paired observations, where two teachers observe the same events and write independent descriptions, are also used.

All observations, done individually or in pairs, are followed by group discussion; it is in these discussions that the group members begin to move from description to analysis, and to generate new questions for exploration. The pack contains useful support material for this discussion work, with brief readings and examples of teachers' work with the six questions.

If you decide to use some or all of the *Curriculum in Action* pack, there is another point to consider: the questions appear, at face value, to be very simple. If they are treated lightly, by group members who are not yet prepared for the sometimes painful process of critical self-evaluation, they may be used as a way of confirming current practices, and evading the possibility of change and development. It is only when tackled in a genuine spirit of enquiry, coupled with a readiness to be sometimes less than self-satisfied, that the six questions can have a dramatic effect on attitudes and behaviour. It is the crucial task of the group leader to encourage the members to adopt a critical approach to their own practice.

* Open University (1981)
Curriculum in Action: an Approach to Evaluation
P234, Open University pubs.

The *Curriculum in Action* pack is based on six deceptively simple questions. They invite you to make a series of observations in your place of work with children. The questions are:

what were the children actually doing?

what were they learning?

how worthwhile was it?

what did you (the adult) do?

what did you learn?

what will you do next?

Don't be misled by the everyday language of the questions into thinking that the answers are quick and simple. They are not easy to answer. Indeed the longer you think about them the more complicated they can become. Each question and the explorations you need to make to answer it lead to other questions and further explorations.

QUESTION 1.

What were the children actually doing?

This question seems to be about observation - 'if I look carefully at the room where I work I will see what happens to the children there'. However, the question is also about your good intentions and what happens to them - do you see what you were hoping to see? Are the children doing what you intended them to do? After two or three detailed observations with these questions in mind, you will probably find the relationship between your curriculum (your plans, hopes, fears) and the children's curriculum (what actually happens) is not a simple one. How does your interpretation (and selective memory) of events relate to the children's version? Can you get closer to seeing what they see, experiencing what they experience?

QUESTION 2.

What were the children learning?

Answering this question can be an uncomfortable experience for any adult responsible for young children. Can we ever be certain that we know what the children were learning? We might ask with more confidence, what might the children have been learning? There will always be intended and unintended learning for the children, since you cannot exercise total control over what a child learns even if you are physically present, or providing the equipment, or asking all the questions ... What sort of evidence are you looking for? How will you know that a child has learned something? What will it look like? Armed with these related questions, adults can turn again to the process of observation.

After another round of observations with the concept of *learning* in mind, it is time to ask more questions. If you do not have the evidence of learning that you were looking for is it because you do not give the children the opportunity to express their learning? How many and what kind of opportunities do the children have to show what they have learned and put it into action? What does this say about the room where you work and what the adults do in it?

QUESTION 3.

How worthwhile was it?

This seems to be a 'how' question, but underneath it is a relentless series of 'why?' questions. You hope the learning was worthwhile, but why? What leads you to believe this? You can list the elements of the activity or the learning that seem to you to be worthwhile, but why? What leads you to give them that value or assign that priority? By asking 'why?' about taken-for-granted beliefs and values, you may gain insight into your 'curriculum in action' and what underlies it. Will you judge this to be worthwhile?

QUESTION 4.

What did you, the adult, do?

This question looks safer: it's about people and things, about concrete nouns and what you did to them. You gave a child a toy, you praised a child's construction ... However, the tricky questions start to intrude - what did you leave *undone*, *unsaid*; who amongst the children did you fail to talk with? touch? whose questions did you fail to answer? What is the relationship between what *you* did and what the *children* did? Who and what decided what you did next? You are inevitably making choices at every moment of the day. Do the children's actions modify your choices? Or do your actions modify theirs? And whose room is this anyway?

QUESTION 5.

What did you learn?

QUESTION 6.

What will you do next?

By the time you turn to these last two questions you will have developed a kind of binocular vision. You will have learned a good deal about your own actions, and those of the children you work with. But you will also have learned something about evaluation. As you look more closely at your work, you begin to see more clearly the purposes and consequences of what is happening, and the values that power the enterprise. You have looked at events, and the meaning of events, and have begun to see not only what is happening but why. And what will you do next? Start the cycle again: observe, describe, analyse, reflect. The final message of these six questions is that the process of exploration and reflection is always incomplete.

Activity 8E

AFTER QUESTIONS, WHAT NEXT...?

Time 20 minutes or
the rest of your life

You may find that the questions you chose were too vague, or too general, and that you need to sharpen them up in order to see more clearly what is going on. For example, if you are investigating co-operative play, it is more helpful to look at a couple of children who specially interest you, and ask yourself when, where and how they co-operate, than to try to observe co-operation whenever it takes place.

So the next stage after asking questions can sometimes be: asking more questions.

But perhaps the questions you asked have given you a wealth of material to think about and discuss. You may be stimulated to alter some aspect of your provision (change the rules, introduce new equipment, increase adult involvement in a certain activity). Or you may use your observations to help you write some kind of policy statement for your work place about the topic you have been researching.

IN WORKING THROUGH THIS SECTION YOU WILL HAVE

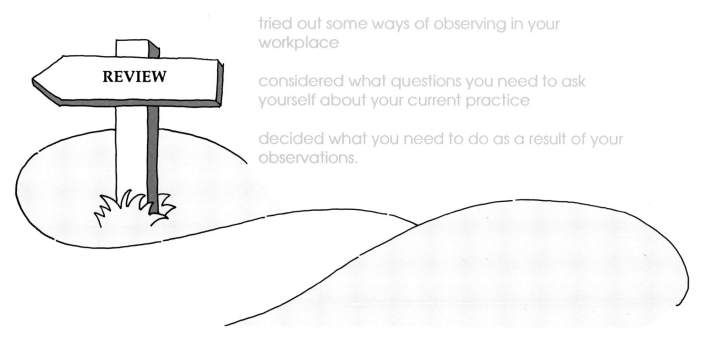

tried out some ways of observing in your workplace

considered what questions you need to ask yourself about your current practice

decided what you need to do as a result of your observations.

81

Section 9
MOVING FROM AIMS TO PRACTICE

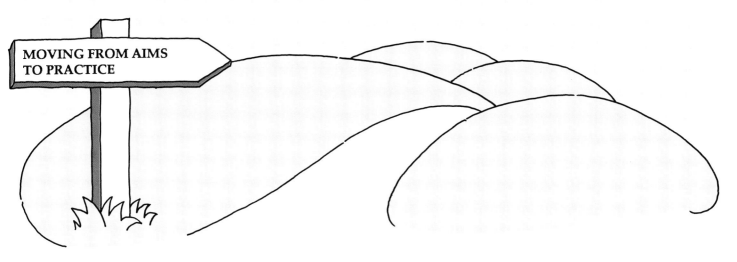

MOVING FROM AIMS
TO PRACTICE

IN WORKING THROUGH THIS SECTION YOU WILL BE ABLE TO

identify the overall aims you are working towards

identify the goals through which you will achieve these aims, and make some plans for achieving the goals

discuss ways of checking that you are making progress towards achieving your aims

decide with colleagues what you could write down about your curriculum and who would use what you have written.

USERS' COMMENTS

'We found this the most important part of the pack, but we were glad to have done other sections first'.

'A tremendous challenge - it really clarified our thinking'.

'The group needed a lot of support and encouragement to persist with this difficult but challenging and worthwhile section'.

This section is about helping you to make a detailed curriculum plan that makes sense to you and everyone else in your work place.

Discussion and thinking time can lead to a plan that not only makes more sense to the people involved in creating it but is also clear enough to be communicated confidently to parents or to colleagues in related professions. If the details are not clear, or we lack confidence in what we do, then conversations that open with 'Tell me what do you really do all day?' or 'Tell me what is the point of my child coming here?' will be a source of anxiety.

In developing a curriculum plan for ourselves, we need to ask

> where are we going?

> how shall we get there?

> how shall we know that we are moving forward?

Discussions of aims and objectives often come to grief because 'where are we going' (on which there may be agreement) has been confused with 'how shall we get there?' (about which there is considerable disagreement).

So, the first question is

> where are we going?

There are two parts to this question

> what are our overall aims?

> and

> what are the goals through which we will achieve our aims?

Overall aims do not have to be specific. Perhaps you will have five or six broad aims, which can be used later to work out clear goals .
The wording of overall aims leaves room for different interpretations, while goals should be worked out in such a way that they are clear to everyone and cannot be misinterpreted.

84

1 What are our overall aims?

Activity 9A

DESIGN A POSTER

PREPARATION	Paper and pencils. Flip chart or large paper if you wish to share individual work in the group.
NOTE TO GROUP LEADERS	This activity tends to work better when group members work with colleagues from their own or similar work places.

ACTIVITY *

1 Working in pairs or small groups imagine that you have to design a poster that will be fixed by the front door of your establishment. The poster will be weatherproof and built to last five years. You have a limit of 15 words to sum up the work of your establishment. It is a public statement about 'this is us and what we are here for'. Your words must include 'we' and must not include words like 'try' or 'perhaps'. You can use this statement as your overall aim that you continue with in the following activities.

2. Come together as a group to share your posters.

FOLLOW UP

You could use this activity to help you work out your overall aim for every aspect of children's learning. For example, sum up in 15 words what you want children to achieve in the brick corner.

* (This activity comes from *Working with young children*, Laishley 1987).

85

2 What are the goals through which we will achieve these aims?

The next step is to identify the specific goals that will help us achieve our aims.

Activity 9B

DEFINING GOALS
                                                               Time several sessions
                                                               of 45 minutes

PREPARATION   Paper and pencils. Copies of the SOAPIT handout for the
                           group to discuss

NOTE TO GROUP LEADERS   Reaching good workable goals is not easy. It usually takes
                           several attempts, some pointed asking of 'but what will it
                           look like?' or 'how will you do it?' or 'why will you do it?' It
                           will also require discussion - and possibly argument - in a
                           team.

ACTIVITY   Working in pairs take one of your overall aims and ask
                           yourselves 'How would we recognise this when
                           we see it?'

                           For example, if the overall aim is
                           'We want to create an environment where children can
                           take responsibility for their own learning'
                           you might ask yourselves the question 'what would it look
                           like if we had created an environment where children
                           were taking responsibility for their own learning?'

                           As a first draft of goals, you might came up with the
                           following:-

                           *Children would be able to operate
                           independently*

                           Children would be free to choose

                           Children would be offered a varied experience

                           Children would develop a sense of responsibility

                           *Children would be encouraged to develop self confi-
                           dence*

                       2. The next stage is to take each of these goals and ask
                           'What would this look like in practice?' Don't be afraid of
                           being very specific - for example 'children will be expected
                           to put away equipment they have taken out when they
                           have finished using it' or 'children will have access to
                           woodwork with saws and hammers and nails every day'.

                       3   After working in pairs, come together for discussion in the
                           full group. You may find the SOAPIT handout useful at this
                           stage.

HANDOUT 9B

SOAPIT: a guide to writing goals

WORTHWHILE GOALS NEED TO BE

Specific

Observable

Achievable

Performance related

Involving

Time bound

SOAPIT is a useful way of remembering some tough criteria for setting goals.

Worthwhile goals are

specific so that everyone can have a shared understanding of what is meant.

observable so that we can see whether they are being achieved or not.

achievable or else disillusionment and depression can lie ahead.

related to doing, to performing and not just with trying or hoping. For example, it is not a worthwhile goal for staff to agree to try to deal in a given manner with any racist remarks made by children. The workable goal is that staff actually do this on every occasion.

involving people in making them, or there will be little effort put in.

on a realistic time scale of achievement and monitoring.

If you find these criteria difficult, don't despair. Take them one at a time, and think about why it seems so challenging. For example, if you are getting nowhere with how to make your goals observable, is it because of who else might do the observing? Are you worried that parents will be able to observe your shortcomings? Would they be critical? How does this make you feel? Talking through why the criteria are too difficult to put into practice, may help you and your colleagues overcome feelings of defensiveness or anxiety.

When you have commited yourselves to a list of workable and worthwhile goals you can ask the next question.

3 How shall we get there?

This asks about the plans we could make to set about achieving
our goals. This is not the time to seize the nearest curriculum pack
or local guidelines and say 'This seems close enough, let's go'.

Activity 9C

REVIEWING RESOURCES AND ROLES   Time 30-40 minutes
                                                                  for each goal

PREPARATION   Paper and pencils. A note of the goals you identified
                          in 9B.

ACTIVITY

1   Working in pairs or small groups of 3 - 4, take the goals you identified in 9B one at
    a time and consider what factors will influence the plans you make to achieve
    each one.

    They may be influenced by the children you have - their age, previous experience
    etc. The *resources* at your disposal will also influence you. Consider what you have in:

    People resources - time available (people hours), the skills, the energy
    Space resources - square metres, number of rooms, access to further space
    Equipment - the play materials and equipment, the stocks of consumables like paper
    Finance- existing funds and the ease of fund-raising

    Your work place will have its own package of resources and it is important not to
    concentrate on the apparent negatives ('We don't have a spare - room, so we can't.
    . . ') at the cost of the positive ('We have parents from six different ethnic groups, so
    we can call on knowledge of ... and skills. . . ')

    Let us take an example from earlier. The overall aim was 'we want to create an
    environment where children can take responsibility for their own learning'.

    Perhaps one of the goals linked with this aim has been identified as being 'All drawers
    and cupboards will be clearly marked with pictures so that children can select and
    tidy away equipment independently'. To achieve this goal you need to consider the
    resources you have:

    People - which people would be willing/able to make labels?
    Space -is the available space organised in a way that encourages children to open
    cupboards or look on shelves, or do you need to re-organise?
    - how much can you do if your storage area is not accessible to children?
    Equipment -what storage space do you have? Are there enough cupboards, trays,
    shelves, containers? What else do you need?
    Finance -what will the extra storage equipment cost? Have you enough money?

2   Now, consider *who* is going to do it? Every route to achieving a goal will have
    implications for the *role* that adults - staff and parents and others - will need to take on.

3   Look back again to your goals, and ask yourself for each one how can we make this
    happen? what needs doing? who will do it? when will they do it? where and how will
    they do it? will it affect other things that they do at present?

4. How will we know we are moving forward?

This question is about how we judge whether we are making progress. We will not reach a final end point, for goals will only be achieved over a period of time, with some children and in some areas of work. We need to be able to evaluate how well we are doing at any one time. If our goals are specific and observable, this should not be too difficult.

There will also be lessons to learn from relative success and failure. With different children, different staff, on different days there will always be unexpected progress and unexpected difficulties.

Actiivity 9D

MONITORING PROGRESS

Time 30-45 minutes at a time.
Several sessions required

PREPARATION
Paper and pencils. Flip chart or large paper. Notes from Activities 9B and 9C.

NOTE TO GROUP LEADERS
This activity will take a considerable amount of time - more than a single session if it is done properly. It is best done after the other activities in section 9.

ACTIVITY

1   Working with the whole group go back to your goals (Activity 9B) and look at the possible ways you opted to achieve them (Activity 9C).
How can you monitor your progress? What could you do to make sure you are achieving your goals?
Share ideas on ways of checking you are making progress, using a flip chart, or large sheet of paper.

2   Consider which ideas you could most easily put into practice. Which ideas would best give you the information you need to enable you to see whether you are making progress?
At the end of this discussion you should as a group be able to write down some clear ideas for monitoring progress.

3   Now that you have your goals clearly written down, as well as ideas for ensuring your goals are put into practice, and ideas for monitoring progress, you need to decide

Who will see and read this work? All staff? Parents?

Where will it be kept?

Who will have access to it and use it? Will parents be involved?

How will you keep it up to date?

89

IN WORKING THROUGH THIS SECTION YOU WILL HAVE

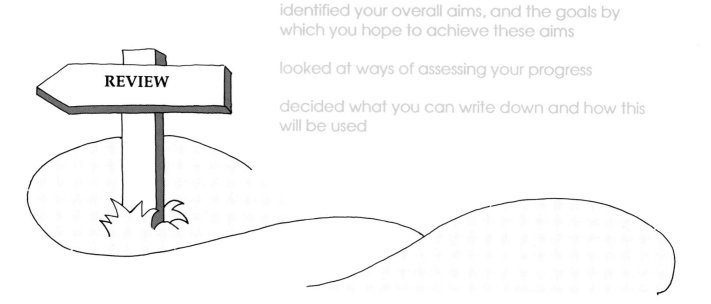

identified your overall aims, and the goals by which you hope to achieve these aims

looked at ways of assessing your progress

decided what you can write down and how this will be used

Section 10
LOOKING BACK, LOOKING AHEAD

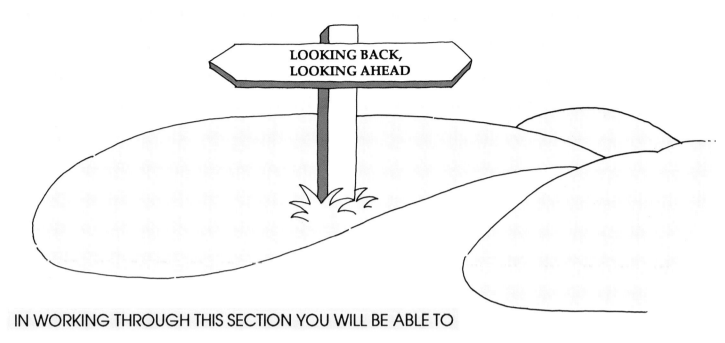

IN WORKING THROUGH THIS SECTION YOU WILL BE ABLE TO

- review the work you have done on the pack, both individually and as a member of a group

- reflect on the ways in which your practice has been or will be affected

- consider how your thinking about young children and your own work with them has been influenced by the discussions and activities you have been involved in

- prepare to start on the next stage of the never-ending process of learning about learning.

USERS COMMENTS

'We found it helpful to leave a bit of time in between finishing our course and doing this section.'

THE LUXURY OF REFLECTION

In our busy working lives it may seem difficult to justify 'time out' - time to stand back and reflect - not necessarily on the meaning of life - but on the meaning and importance of all the activities that make up each working day.

This section is intended to support you and your colleagues in just such a process, encouraging you to allow yourselves some quiet, peaceful time for reflection. Many of us were taught, as we grew up, that our time was most usefully spent in looking after and attending to the needs of others: this may be one reason why it isn't always easy to secure some time for thinking about ourselves and our own concerns. This need not be in any way a selfish occupation: it can be both challenging and enriching, stimulating, and reassuring. It can help us to appreciate the strengths that we bring to our work, as well as being a step towards thinking about our weaknesses. It can be a private way of celebrating our achievements. It can be the beginning of the next stage of our learning.

Activity 10A

REVIEWING YOUR WORK WITH THE PACK   Time 30-45 minutes

PREPARATION
Copies of the incomplete sentences given below for each group member.

ACTIVITY
1   Working alone, somewhere quiet and free from interruptions, complete the following
    sentences. Feel free to add any other comments of your own.

When we started working on this pack I felt...

I remember saying...

I remember wishing ...

I wondered why...

In my workplace at that time...

My colleagues...

After a few sessions I felt...

I began to...

I thought...

I noticed that...

I particularly remember...

In my workplace I...

My colleagues...

I worried about...

I appreciated...

Now we have finished working on the pack I feel...

I still wonder about...

I think I have learned...

Each section of the pack...

I know I...

In my workplace I...

My colleagues...

Now I know I can...

I wish I hadn't...

I will never forget...

2   Working in twos or threes, share as much of what you have written as you want to with other
    members of the group who have also reviewed their experiences in this way.

Activity 10B

WHAT NEXT?

Time 30 minutes or as long
as you have got

PREPARATION

Copies of the sentences given below for each group member.

ACTIVITY

This is the moment to start thinking about what the next step will be for you, for your colleagues in the group and/or your workplace. The questions below may be a useful talking point for discussion and for forward planning

What do I want to do

think

say

read

talk about

investigate

explore

next?   Why?

Who do I want to do it with?

two or three people

a larger group

the whole of this group

other people I work with?   Why?

When do I want to do it -

tomorrow

next week

next month

next summer

next year?   Why?

Finally what about my colleagues? What are their responses to questions of What, Who, When and Why? Can I help them in any way?

FOLLOW-UP

This is where you set off on your own, with or without your
colleagues. But remember, small steps are less tiring than trying to
run uphill carrying a heavy weight on your back. The three golden
rules of curriculum development were once defined as

think slow

think small

do not call in an expert

YOU CAN DO IT!

Section 11
BIBLIOGRAPHY AND RESOURCES

BIBLIOGRAPHY AND RESOURCES

This short selection of books has been divided into sections in an attempt to make it easier for you to find the titles you are looking for. But, inevitably,the sections overlap, and so some books appear more than once. And, like all selections, this one has gaps and omissions, and does not pretend to be exhaustive. It is best to treat it as a starting point for your particular interests.
More extensive and specialised bibliographies are available from the Under Fives Unit, National Children's Bureau, 8 Wakley Street, London ECIV 7QE.
Publications lists are also available from organisations such as:

BAECE, 111 City View, 463 Bethnal Green Road, London E2 9QH.
National Childminding Association, 8 Masons Hill, Bromley, Kent BR2 9EY.
Preschool Playgroups Association, 61-63 Kings Cross Road, London WCIX 9LL.
VOLCUF, 77 Holloway Road, London N7 8JZ.

THE GREAT TRADITION

These books may be useful if you choose to undertake the activities in section 5 (Why do we do what we do?) that are based on the work of the pioneers in the field of early childhood. (Other useful titles are referred to in the text of section 5).

Bradburn, E   (1989)   *Margaret McMillan: Portrait of a Pioneer*   Routledge and Kegan Paul.

Bruce, T   (1987)   *Early Childhood Education*   Hodder and Stoughton.

Deasey, D   (1978)   *Education Under Six*   Croom Helm.

Isaacs, S   (1930)   *Intellectual Growth in Young Children*   Routledge and Kegan Paul.

McMillan, M   (1919)   *The Nursery School*   Dent.

RESEARCH STUDIES AND REVIEWS

Clark, M M   (1988)   *Children Under Five: Educational Research and Evidence*   Gordon and Breach.

Donaldson, M   (1978)   *Children's Minds*   Fontana/Collins.

Osborn, A & Milbank, J   (1987)   *The Effects of Early Education*   Oxford, ClarendonPress.

Rutter, M   (1981)   *Maternal Deprivation Reassessed*   Penguin 2nd edition.

Sylva, K, Roy, C & Painter, M   (1980)   *Childwatching in Playgroup and Nursery*   Grant McIntyre.

Tizard, B   (1986)   *The Care of Young Children - Implications of Recent Research*   Thomas Coram Research Unit.

Tizard, B et al   (1988)   *Young Children at School in the Inner City*   Lawrence Erlbaum Associates.

CHILD DEVELOPMENT

Pringle, M K (1986) *The Needs of Children* Hutchinson, 3rd edition.

Roberts, M & Tamburrini, J (1981) *Child Development 0 - 5* Holmes McDougall.

This is a fully illustrated and very readable basic text on all aspects of child development. If you are specially interested in the development of language, these titles may be useful:

Tizard, B & Hughes, M (1984) *Young Children Learning* Fontana.

Tough, J (1974) *Focus on Meaning* Allen and Unwin.

Wells, G (1986) *The Meaning Makers* Hodder and Stoughton.

Wood, D (1988) *How Children Think and Learn* Basil Blackwell.

PARENTS AND YOUNG CHILDREN

De'Ath, E & Pugh, G (eds) (1987) *Working with Parents: a Training Resource Pack* National Children's Bureau.

Pugh, G & De'Ath, E (1984) *The Needs of Parents: Practice and Policy in Parent Education* Macmillan.

Pugh, G & De'Ath, E (1989) *Working Towards Partnership in the Early Years* National Children's Bureau.

Scarr, S & Dunn, J (1987) *MotherCare OtherCare* Penguin.

Smith, T (1980) *Parents and Preschool* Grant McIntyre.

Tizard, B et al (1981) *Involving Parents in Nursery and Infant School* Grant McIntyre.

PRE-SCHOOL SETTINGS FOR WORK WITH YOUNG CHILDREN

Bryant B, Harris M, & Newton D, (1980) *Children & Minders* Grant McIntyre.

Crowe, B (1974) *Playgroup Activities: What, Why, How?* Preschool Playgroups Association

Donaghue, J (1983) *Running a Mother and Toddler Group* Allen & Unwin.

Garland, C & White S, (1980) *Children and Day Nurseries* Grant McIntyre.

Gilkes, J (1987) *Developing Nursery Education* Open University Press (an account of the work of a joint centre for pre-school children).

Henderson, A & Lucas, J (1981) *Pre-school Playgroups: a Handbook* Allen& Unwin.

Laishley, J (1987) *Working with Young Children: a Handbook* Edward Arnold 2nd edition

McNaughton, G et al (1986) *Working Together: Good Practice Guidelines for GLC/ILEA day nurseries* GLC.

Pugh, G (1988) *Services for Under Fives: Developing a Co-ordinated Approach* National Children's Bureau.

YOUNG CHILDREN AT SCHOOL

Barrett, G   (1986)   *Starting School: An Evaluation of the Experience*   Assistant Masters and Mistresses Association.

Blatchford, P, Battle, S & Mays, J   (1982)   *The First Transition: Home to Pre-School*   NFER Nelson

Bruce, T   (1987)   *Early Childhood Education*   Hodder and Stoughton.

Cleave, S, Jowett, S & Bate, M   (1982)   *And So to School*   NFER Nelson.

NFER/SCDC   (1987)   *Four Year Olds in School: Policy and Practice*   NFER.

THE EARLY YEARS CURRICULUM

These books are expressly concerned with the curriculum offered in educational settings.

Blenkin, G & Kelly, A V (eds)   (1988)   *Early Childhood Education: a Developmental Curriculum*   Paul Chapman.

Bruce, T   (1987)   *Early Childhood Education*   Hodder and Stoughton.

Curtis, A   (1986)   *A Curriculum for the Pre-School Child: Learning to Learn*   NFER/Nelson.

Department of Education and Science   (1985)   *The Curriculum 5 - 16: Curriculum Matters 2*   HMS0.

Dowling, M   (1988)   *Education 3 - 5: A Teacher's Handbook*   Paul Chapman.

Gammage, P   (1982)   *Children and Schooling*   Allen and Unwin.

Manning, K & Sharp, A   (1977)   *Structuring Play in the Early Years at School*   Ward Lock.

National Association of Inspectors & Education Advisers   (1986)   *The Needs of 3 - 5 year olds*

Tough, J   (1976)   *Listening to Children Talking*   Ward Lock.

Tough, J   (1977)   *Talking and Learning*   Ward Lock.

EQUAL OPPORTUNITIES

Adams, C   (ed) (1986)   *Primary Matters*   ILEA (accounts by teachers of anti-racist and anti-sexist initiatives in primary schools).

Aspinwall, K A   (1984)   *What are Little Girls Made Of? What are Little Boys Made Of?*   National Nursery Examination Board.

Durrant, J & Kidner, J   (1988)   *'Racism and the under fives'* in Cohen A and Cohen L (eds)   *Early Education: the Pre-School Years*   Paul Chapman.

Equal Opportunities Commission   (1986)   *An Equal Start: Guidelines for Those Working With Under Fives*   EOC.

Grabrucker, M   (1988)   *There's a Good Girl: Gender Stereotyping in the First Three Years of Life: a diary*
The Women's Press.

Milner, D   (1983)   *Children & Race: Ten Years on*   Ward Lock Educational

Moss, P   (1988)   *Childcare and Equality of Opportunity*   Commissionof the European Communities.

VOLCUF   (1986)   *Anti-racist Childcare - Pack of Information*   VOLCUF.

Bibliographies on *Childcare in a multi-racial society* and *Anti-sexist childcare practice/sex role stereotyping in young children* are available from the Under Fives Unit at the National Children's Bureau, 8 Wakley Street, London ECIV 9QE.

TRAINING PACKS

De'Ath, E & Pugh, G (eds) (1987) *Working with Parents: a Training Resource Pack* National Children's Bureau.

Open University *Childminding P971* Open University Publications.

Open University *Living with Babies and Toddlers P961C* Open University Publications

Open University *The Preschool Child P912C* Open University Publications.

Open University *Women & Young Children: Learning Through Experience P593* Open University Publications.

Open University *Parents Talking: The Developing Child P596* Open University Publications.

Open University (1981) *Curriculum in Action: an Approach to Evaluation P234* Open University Publications.

Some of these training packs emphasise the importance of close observation of young children; another useful title on the topic of observation is:

Laishley, J (1987) (revised edition) *Working with Young Children* Edward Arnold.

BOOKS ABOUT CHILDREN

Lastly, a brief selection of books about real live children!

Axline, V (1986) *Dibs: in search of self* Penguin.

Berg, L *Looking at Kids*

Crowe, B (1980) *Living with a Toddler* Allen & Unwin.

Grabrucker, M (1988) *There's a good girl: gender stereotyping in the first three years of life: a diary* The Women's Press.

Paley, V (1981) *Wally's Stories* Harvard University Press (and other titles by the same author: *Molly is Three, Bad Guys Don't Have Birthdays* etc).